NURSES
BEHIND BARS

You Can't Make This Stuff Up

BETH GRAYSON

authorHOUSE®

AuthorHouse™
1663 Liberty Drive
Bloomington, IN 47403
www.authorhouse.com
Phone: 833-262-8899

Published by AuthorHouse 09/28/2022

ISBN: 978-1-6655-6294-2 (sc)
ISBN: 978-1-6655-6293-5 (e)

Library of Congress Control Number: 2022911502

Written material based on real events. The names
have been changed to protect the incarcerated.

This book is dedicated to my loving mom. She is the most wonderful woman I have ever known in my life. Mom has always been there for me through all the good times and the hardest times. She is my heart. I love you more than you could ever know.

CONTENTS

Upon leaving my home fifteen minutes earlier than usual, I am feeling proud of myself, thinking I'll get to work in plenty of time. That feeling doesn't last long. When I make a left turn to go beneath the railroad underpass, I come upon a line of traffic.

It is backing up behind a semitruck with another semitruck loaded on its flatbed. The truck is inching forward and appears too tall to get through the clearly posted "thirteen foot clearance" sign.

Some smart person, a few cars ahead of me, finally figures out to make a U-turn, and we all follow suit. I head for the road that goes around the city and finally end up on the highway, heading south to work. Then there is something up ahead. Of course, a train! So there I sit again, trying to relax, when my irritable bowel syndrome kicks in. Stress or road rage tends to do that. Finally, the coal train rambles away, and the crossing arms rise. I cross the railroad tracks, thinking it's smooth sailing now.

I think that I should say, "The glass is half full," but then I see a lot of orange pylons and signs that say there is road construction. That glass is looking emptier by the minute. I finally get through the bumps of the dirt road and make it to the highway turnoff. At the next stop sign is one of the biggest bulldozers I've ever seen. The driver can't get enough speed to make it across the highway due to traffic.

Eventually, I make my left turn and am on my way. Traffic is snailing along. When the opportunity finally presents itself, I put the pedal to the metal. I fly by all the slow-moving cars and trucks at about ninety-five miles per hour. I feel the adrenaline kick in, and my heart races in my chest.

Ahead, just a few miles from my destination, the same semitruck loaded with a semitruck is ahead of me. With an even greater burst of irritation, I burn right past it. I usually can keep my road rage to myself, but not this morning.

I finally get to work at the all-female prison and relay my sad story of events to one of my nursing staff. Once she finishes laughing, she informs me that today is Friday the thirteenth. I have a newfound respect for believing in superstitions.

I get into my office and review the agenda for the day. I'm ready to face all the unhappy and often very difficult inmates, with their medical issues. I'm the medical director of a female prison. I fall into my chair, hoping that I'd taken all my blood pressure medications this morning.

★ ★ ★

I was born and raised in a town of about twenty thousand people. I guess you'd say I had a pretty protected upbringing. Aside from going to school, I was sent to church Sunday mornings, Sunday evenings, Wednesdays after school, and Wednesday evenings.

I wasn't allowed to go to movies or dances, and I couldn't date until I was eighteen years old. At eighteen, I went to the neighborhood university and became a registered nurse. I built my career working in all areas of the nursing field, to be as diverse and experienced as I could get.

It was a very safe and perhaps overly protected childhood. So who would've guessed I'd end up in prison? Well, about twenty seasoned years later, I did.

There is one thing to be said about working in a women's prison. There is no such thing as redundancy and boredom—it's quite the opposite. No day is like the day before. And to quote a phrase from a well-known movie, "Life is like a box of chocolates. You never know what you're gonna get."

CHAR

Char was always a good kid. In high school, she was captain of the varsity cheerleading squad and cocaptain of the volleyball team. At five feet eleven inches, she was the center of the girls' varsity basketball team. Char was active in her church youth group and taught Sunday school to grades one and two.

She held straight As in all her studies. As the oldest child in her family, her four younger siblings all looked up to her. In her junior year, she was nominated prom queen. After high school, Char planned to become a veterinarian. Everything was great.

On prom night, she and her date, the football team's quarterback, went to an after-prom party at a local hotel. She had a couple of beers, and her date was doing shots with his buddies. Char eventually told Tom it was time to go home.

He resisted and soon became angry at her persistence to leave. He finally relented, and they headed to the parking lot. Once in the car, he lost his temper and told her that he was sick of her goody-two-shoes ways. The more Char tried to calm him down, the angrier he became.

His eyes grew very dark, and he said he was going to have a good time no matter what she said. Tom ripped at her beautiful dress and pulled down her underwear. He raped her that night in the front seat of his car.

Char didn't remember the drive home or even getting to her bedroom. She got into the shower and sobbed for a long time under the scathing hot water. When she awoke the next morning, it felt like it was just a nightmare. But when she used the bathroom, the bloody tissue told her it had been very real.

She changed after that night. Her grades began slipping, as did her efforts and attitudes with all her extracurricular activities. She began skipping school and quit her Sunday school position. She started hanging with the type of crowd she used to feel sorry for—the teens who drank during lunch hour and used drugs.

She started with alcohol, but it wasn't long before she used much harder drugs. She was failing in her senior year and finally dropped out. Her parents couldn't figure out the night and day changes that occurred with their daughter. Over time, even her family gave up on trying to figure her out.

She began stealing from her parents and even her brother and sisters to get her fix. She was addicted to meth and heroin. Char lost a great deal of weight and was only eighty-five pounds. By the time she was twenty years old, she had three DUIs, two possession charges, multiple shoplifting charges, and driving under suspension charges.

And she had two children under the age of five. Neither child knew their father. Char's parents kicked her out of their home and started raising her two children. She moved in with her thirty-one-year-old boyfriend, who was also heavily addicted to drugs. He held down a part-time job, which paid for their drug use but left little money for food and rent.

On her last day of freedom, Char purchased three grams of meth and four chunks of heroin from an undercover agent. She was taken to jail and sentenced to five years in prison. On her arrival to prison, she was skin and bone and had multiple sores over her body that hadn't healed.

She was verbally abusive during her intake physical and called staff everything, from cops to motherfuckers to fucking niggers. She was removed from the intake area and taken to a solitary confinement cell until she calmed down and was willing to cooperate. She stayed in the hole (common slang for solitary confinement) for five days, until she had calmed down enough to complete her medical physical.

Char continued to be a difficult inmate for the first year of her imprisonment. She had no interest in making friends but did make a lot of enemies. She learned to stick with the toughest gang on her unit, who would watch her back for her, and she in turn for them.

One of her gang mates tattooed her neck with the words "Fuck 'Em." Char was treated in the medical department for the badly infected tattoo. She got in a lot of fights, sometimes just for the sport of it. One night, when she jumped Viv for talking to the correctional officers (COs), the beatdown went too far.

Char ended up stabbing Viv with a sharpened pencil three times in the abdomen. Viv was taken to the ER and required surgery to repair her colon. Char not only spent forty-five days in the hole but also received an additional sentence for assault, which added time to her stay at the prison.

Part of her time was supposed to be spent attaining her GED. It seemed she was purposefully failing her classes, as though it wasn't cool to be smart. Her teacher tried to get through to her, to encourage her to give just a little effort. Those attempts fell on deaf ears.

Signs were posted in all housing units that a religious retreat was going to be held over a weekend next month. It was known that at these retreats, there was lots of good food served to the inmates. Char decided to sign up.

She blew off most of the "religious crap" stuffed down her throat. But there was one counselor at the event who had a connection with her. In the weeks and months following the retreat, the counselor made frequent trips to the prison to lead a Bible study with the inmates.

Amazingly, over time, this counselor's connection with Char paid off. She began improving with her GED studies and her behavior as well. Six months after her first religious retreat, Char had attained her GED certification, had no further write-ups, and lived in the honor dorm. What a changed girl from the drug-addicted, troubled young woman who had walked into the prison's doors not so long ago.

KELLIE

Kellie was a fifty-year-old inmate whose husband was incarcerated as well for selling drugs. She used big words when she talked and had a very strong superiority complex with the inmates as well as the staff. Kellie decided to be a difficult handful the day she arrived at the women's prison. She referred to herself as a "princess who always gets what she wants. One way or another." Unfortunately for Kellie, it didn't quite go her way when she went to court for sentencing on an additional charge that hadn't been settled prior to her incarceration. She truly believed that she would get a slap on the wrist and be sent home after serving two years on her first crime, but it didn't go that way. Kellie received an additional twelve years to serve. The only ones who felt worse than she did were all the staff at the prison who were going to have to deal with her over the next fourteen years. The prison staff weren't happy to think about the upcoming years of Kellie's superiority, bad attitude, and manipulative behaviors.

Just last week, Kellie was escorted to the infirmary by an officer. She had convinced the officer that she was having a stroke and a heart attack at the same time. I asked Kellie why she was allowed to be sent directly to the infirmary instead of following the process of asking a CO to call the medical team prior to the inmate showing up. She first told me that the staff made her come to see medical. When I asked who that staff member was, she changed the subject. I asked her again, and she decided to confess that she had initiated an emergency visit. She excitedly reported that she was having a stroke and that the left side of her body was numb and paralyzed. As I listened and observed Kellie going on and on about her stroke, I noted that she was using both hands

4

raised up in the air to express herself, and her face showed no sign of drooping or weakness and no slurred speech. She was walking around normally as well.

I firmly told her that I didn't believe she was having a stroke. That was when she got mad. She demanded to be sent back downstairs to her cell to call her family and her lawyer. Laura, a staff nurse, talked her into having a seat in the exam room for an assessment. It is really interesting to watch inmates try to outsmart diagnostic equipment such as a blood pressure machine and trained nursing staff. She kept tensing up her muscles on her affected side to try to show a change from her left arm to her right, in an attempt to prove that something was indeed wrong. It was amusing but ineffective. Laura informed me that everything the inmate could not fake during the assessment was completely normal. The things she could fake—for example, hand grip strength—were very exaggerated. I directed Laura to admit Kellie to the infirmary with fifteen-minute vital sign checks and neurological assessments to make sure she was not having a stroke. When Laura told her she was going to be admitted to the infirmary, Kellie became very angry, stating, "You're not throwing me in a hole! Let me go back to my room and call my family and my lawyer!" After that outburst, Kellie stormed out of the infirmary with hands and fists shaking in the air. Watching her tear out of the infirmary again confirmed that there was no observable symptoms of a stroke such as weakness or paralysis.

One helpful thing when dealing with inmates such as Kellie in a prison setting is that there are cameras recording almost everywhere. I later viewed the camera footage before, during, and after Kellie's emergency visit to the infirmary. There were no signs of a stroke ever observed at any time.

Just a few hours later, at lunchtime medication line, Kellie slowly crawled and dragged herself up the stairs to the medical department to receive her noon medications. When she approached medline, she was trying very hard to make one side of her mouth droop down, she was dragging her left leg behind her like a hundred-pound weight, and she couldn't lift her left arm to get her pills to her mouth. In fact, the officer posting at medline poured her glass of water for her because she appeared she couldn't possibly do that herself.

Once in the inmate dining room (IDR), it was observed on camera footage that she seemed to be enjoying her lunch. She was shoveling her food into her mouth with both hands as fast as she could. She looked like she was not about to let any other inmate decide to share her food.

Kellie's exaggerated left-side "paralysis" continued when staff were present throughout the next day. Kellie's goal had not yet been attained. She wanted a ride to the ER, where she could obtain pain medications, all the pudding she could eat, and a chance for escape. When it became clear that I was not sending her to the hospital, her symptoms completely disappeared.

A mere two days later, Kellie came to the medical department complaining of pink eye. The nurse's assessment showed that the eye was reddened, but so was the skin around the eye, and there was no drainage to indicate conjunctivitis. Excessive rubbing of the eye can break blood vessels in the white of the eye and cause reddened skin surrounding it. Kellie's further attempt to be sent to the eye doctor off-site also failed.

Kellie's superior attitude didn't set well with the other inmates. On one occasion, Kellie became involved in a verbal altercation with another inmate during a volleyball game. The heated argument became physical. The recreation officer called over the radio for back up security staff to assist due to a fight. The facility was placed on lockdown. Both inmates were on the ground, kicking and punching each other. The women were separated, cuffed, and taken to the solitary confinement unit, but not before Kellie screamed to the other inmate that she was going to kill her the first chance she got.

A few days later, I received a memo from Kellie stating that she couldn't see and was going blind. Although I believed that this was just another antic of hers, I had security staff bring her to the infirmary to perform a full eye assessment. She arrived with two COs at her side, she was handcuffed, and her ankles were shackled in chains.

Kellie had been to the optometrist just four months ago, had received new glasses at that time, and tested with a perfect twenty-twenty vision score. I asked her to read the eye chart to test her vision with and without her new glasses. She stated she couldn't read any letters on the chart. Kellie said she couldn't even see the chart on the wall standing just six feet from it. At one point, she stated that the glasses she was wearing weren't the glasses she picked out; she didn't like them and wanted to go back to the optometrist's office to pick out a different colored frame. That was definitely a red flag. After my assessment, the facility's doctor completed his exam. No abnormalities could be found. I then told Kellie that her exam was normal, and it was too soon to go in for another pair of glasses. She would not be getting new glasses at this time. Kellie became enraged and started screaming insults and threats at me. She stated, "I'll make you pay! I swear I'll make you pay!" Security quickly removed her from the infirmary and locked her back down, where she continued screaming and trashing her cell.

Later that same day, she stuffed her towel in the toilet and flooded her cell. She was placed in another cell while staff had to clean and mop up the mess before she could be returned to her assigned cell. The next day, Kellie threatened to starve herself to death, stating she'd make the prison responsible for her death. When each tray of food was passed to her through the food port, she would throw the tray of food against the walls. Her starvation plan lasted four days until she decided she was too hungry to continue and agreed to wash down her walls and floor before the next meal would be offered to her.

When inmates are in solitary, the one thing they have is a lot of time to think. Kellie began monitoring when each CO would walk through the unit to check the safety and security of each inmate. These checks were intended to be random, but Kellie soon realized that one particular CO did her rounds exactly fifteen minutes apart. Kellie had a new plan. She removed the elastic waistband from her pants. Timing it just right, she wrapped the elastic around her throat and her wrist. Then she hooked her arm under the frame of her bed and began choking herself. When the CO made rounds, Kellie was blue from asphyxiation and was nonresponsive. CO Candice radioed staff for a medical emergency in the confinement unit. Candace cut and removed the elastic from Kellie's throat and began CPR. When I arrived within two minutes, I told the captain to radio Control to call for an ambulance, and I applied oxygen by mask. I began an assessment and stopped CPR. She had a pulse and was breathing on her own. Her skin color was pinking up. She was quickly transported to the hospital ER. I followed in my car.

Once the doctor said she was stabilized, I entered the trauma room and went to her side to ask her how she was doing. She looked me in the eye and said, "I told you I'd make you pay, you fucking bitch! I got you financially!"

Kellie was admitted to the intensive care unit for observation and tests for esophageal damage. The nurses reported the next day that she was rude and demanding container after container of pudding and Jell-O. The third day, she was discharged back to her cell in solitary. She was placed on suicide protocol with paper eating utensils, nothing sharp whatsoever, and no bra or elastic in her clothing.

Four days later, Kellie chose to play with her life and did the same thing again. But this time, the officer didn't find her as quickly. When the CO made her rounds, Kellie was blue and frothing at the mouth. CPR was done and a pulse and breathing resumed. She was again sent to the ER by ambulance.

The question was, Where did she get the elastic? It was later found that when she was in the hospital the last time, she convinced an unsuspecting nurse to give her a pair of panties to wear. Kellie removed the elastic from the waistband of the panties and tucked it up into her vagina so it could not be found during the strip search upon her return to the prison. Before she left the hospital after her first "suicide attempt," she was already planning to commit the act again. I wondered how anyone could gamble with her life that easily just to get back at me and the prison—and to get lots of pudding.

MARGARET

Margaret was introduced to drugs at a very young age. Her mother died of a heroin overdose when Margaret was in the first grade. On a sunny afternoon, Margaret walked the five blocks from school to her home. She walked through the house calling out for her mother. When she entered her mother's bedroom, Margaret found her lying on her right side, and she appeared to be sleeping. When the little girl couldn't wake her by shouting, she rolled her mother onto her back and saw the needle sticking out of her right arm. She ran to her eighteen-year-old brother's room and cried to Billy that she couldn't wake up their mother. Billy followed Margaret to their mother's room. When he saw the needle and the white froth coming from her mouth, all he said was, "Shit." He pulled his cell phone from the back pocket of his jeans and dialed 911. Then he called his dad, who was working at the coal mine about five miles away. When the ambulance arrived, the paramedics gave her Narcan to reverse the drug's effects and performed CPR. Their father arrived and followed the ambulance to the hospital in his truck, leaving his children behind. The next time Margaret saw her mother was at the funeral.

In the days to follow, her father, Sam, and Billy began using drugs more than ever before. It began to be a regular occurrence for Margaret to observe her family prepare the heroin and inject it into each other's veins. Sam was missing work and making dangerous mistakes while on duty. His supervisor had already given him several warnings. On Sam's last day at his job, he rolled a scraper down the steep slopes of the dirt road climbing out of the mine. He was high.

The unpaid bills covered the dining room table. Drugs became the priority in their home and often came before food. Margaret went to bed hungry many nights. Her brother and father continued using heavily over the weeks and months, needing more and more as they chased the high.

One night, Margaret heard Sam and Billy yelling in very angry voices. Margaret went to the kitchen and asked her father what was going on. He told her that their drug supplier had screwed them for the last time. Sam said the drugs were watered down so TJ, their dealer, could make more profit. Sam and Billy decided to pay TJ a visit and get what TJ owed them. Margaret was told to drive them to the dealer's house. When the guys went into the house, Margaret was told to sit tight and leave the engine running because this visit should only take a minute.

TJ denied lacing down the heroin and told them to get out. He picked up the .22 gun from the table and pointed it at Sam. Billy pulled his 9mm from the back waistband of his jeans and shot TJ three times in the chest.

When a woman entered the kitchen and saw TJ slumped over in the chair covered in blood, she began screaming. Sam grabbed Billy's arm and shouted, "Run!" They ran to the running car and yelled, "Go, go, fucking go!" Margaret sped for home knowing now was not the time to ask what happened. But she knew.

It wasn't long before the police arrived and took Sam, Billy, and Margaret into custody. All three received many years in prison for the murder of TJ Harris.

Margaret was sentenced to fifteen years in prison for the part she played.

Margaret quickly changed from the sweet and kind girl she once was. She became very cold, and her heart was full of hate. The other inmates knew to stay out of her way. During her first thirty days in the sixteen-bed orientation dorm, she established her reputation several times. On her second day, she decided to take a shower. Both showers were in use. Margaret whipped open the shower curtain, grabbed the girl by the hair, pulled her out of the shower, and threw her to the floor. The inmate stayed on the floor and didn't utter a word until Margaret was in the shower. She then quietly got up, dried herself, wrapped her soapy hair in her towel, and crawled into her bed.

Many of the women learned the importance of knowing when to speak out and when to stay silent. One such inmate, Lindsey, took the beating from Margaret but refused to tell the CO where her black eye and split lip came from. Margaret redecorated Lindsey's face for allegedly stealing her coffee. She plead with Margaret, telling her she didn't do it, but Margaret didn't believe her. Lindsay knew better than to fight back. If she had done so, there would be more to come. An hour after the attack, the coffee was found in a cereal box, where Margaret inadvertently had put it the day before.

On another occasion, Margaret told Sandy to hide her cookies from lunch in a napkin down her shirt to give her when the group returned to their dorms from the cafeteria. When Sandy got to the medium-security housing unit, she was randomly selected for a strip search. The CO found the cookies, which were confiscated and destroyed, and Sandy was given a write-up. But she was worried a lot more about what Margaret was going to do to her than the disciplinary process for stealing from the inmate dining room, (IDR). When Margaret demanded the snack that Sandy couldn't give her, she had to pay the price. Later that same day, two of Margaret's cohorts grabbed Sandy while another was the lookout for staff. They took her to the dorm door. She was held against the wall, and a washcloth was stuffed in her mouth. Margaret grabbed her left arm and put Sandy's hand on the door frame. She then forcefully slammed the door shut on her hand three times, breaking bones in Sandy's hand. The skin of Sandy's index finger broke open and bled profusely, and the middle finger swelled up and turned purple. All Margaret said was, "Keep your fucking mouth shut, or I'll bust the rest of your fucking fingers"! When Sandy couldn't take the pain anymore, she went to the posting CO, showed him her swollen broken hand, and asked to see the nurse. He asked her what had happened. Sandy told him that she fell outside during rec. Despite the CO's insistent questioning about what had really happened, she refused to tell the truth. Upon arrival to the medical department, I also asked her multiple times about what really broke the bones in her hand. Each time, she told me the same thing, but the details were different when I pried into her story. I finally gave up, cleaned and wrapped her wounds, and sent her to the ER for X-rays and treatment. When she returned from the hospital ER, I scheduled her with an orthopedic surgeon to operate and repair her hand. The fractures were not clean breaks but complex fractures that would require pins and plates.

After surgery and ten thousand dollars of taxpayer's money, she returned back to the facility and quietly crawled into bed. This attack was known about by every inmate throughout the prison. No inmate messed with Margaret.

AUTUMN

Autumn was a young Native American woman who frequented our doors. At the age of thirty-one, she arrived at the prison for her third incarceration. Usually her crimes involved drugs, alcohol, and violence. This time, her offense was much more serious.

Autumn and her family got together for an outdoor barbecue on a sunny Sunday afternoon. With all gatherings like this, there was a lot of drinking and partying with her family members. When Autumn drank, her personality changed for the worse. She became angry and violent. On most days where no alcohol or drugs were involved, Autumn was a quiet-mannered girl who talked with a soft, demure voice. But on the Sunday of her crime, the quiet girl drastically changed. During a game of horseshoes, she and her brother, Tony, got into an argument about who got the last point. The argument escalated and became louder. Autumn ran into the kitchen of her aunt's house and grabbed a steak knife. She tore out to the backyard, screaming and yelling at her brother that he was a fucking liar. She grabbed his left shoulder, turned him around to face her, and stabbed him in the belly six times while her family watched. She dropped the knife to the ground, ran to her car, and sped off. Tony lay in the dirt in a fetal position, moaning and bleeding. Uncle Ted called for an ambulance.

After assessment in the ER, he was rushed to surgery, and the team worked to save this twenty-seven-year-old's life before he bled out and died. The doctors worked on him for five hours. Tony survived and spent the next week in the hospital.

Autumn was found by the authorities hiding in the basement of her cousin's home thirty-five miles from the scene of the stabbing. She was arrested and charged with attempted murder. She quietly surrendered to the police, was cuffed and placed in the backseat of the police car, and was taken to jail. Autumn sat in jail for three months awaiting trial. She was sentenced to fifteen years in prison.

The strangest thing observed was that she appeared content to be at the prison again. She stayed in her dorm much of the time reading or watching TV and didn't cause any trouble. Although she seemed comfortable in this setting, which was good, it was sad to see how much of her life she would miss out on in the next fifteen years.

LATESHA

Seated across the desk from me was a new inmate by the name of Latesha. She was a native girl about twenty-four years old dressed in a striped inmate uniform. She gave short, curt answers and was not cooperative. She did not make eye contact. When she decided that the admission interview was over, it was over. I had just asked her if she had any history of HIV or AIDS, and she slammed her fists down on my desk, knocking over pencils and pens, and yelled, "Fuck this shit, and fuck you! I'm not doing this shit!" Then she looked me in the eye. I'll never forget those eyes. It wasn't the brown with flecks of gold, but it was the hatred I saw in them. In my many years dealing with incarcerated men and women, I'd never seen such pure hate.

Security was immediately there to remove her from my office, but she wasn't going to go easily. As she screamed profanities at the staff, three officers struggled with her to get her cuffed and restrained. Latesha fought the officers, kicking and swinging, and she even managed to bite one of the officers' arm before she was restrained and removed from the infirmary. Her medical intake would have to wait. She was placed in a special management unit (SMU) cell, also called disciplinary detention (DD), due to her uncooperative and violent behavior for the night. Staff tried again the next day to complete her admission, but she wasn't having it. She threw her food trays at the walls and at staff through the food port. She urinated in her coffee mug and sprayed that at staff through the port as well. Due to this, she was given only finger foods on paper plates and utensils.

When in SMU, the inmate must uncover their heads on command so the officer can observe that she is all right. Multiple times, staff had to rush her cell with protection suits to do so. Finally, her safety blanket was removed because she would not follow commands to let staff know she was okay. Latesha may have been uncomfortable and cold, but she still was not ready or willing to comply with staff's requirements for her own safety.

This went on for several days until she had finally had enough and told staff that she would comply. Her admission process was completed, and she was placed in the thirty-day orientation dorm with fifteen other ladies. I had real concerns about that, and it didn't take long until my initial concerns proved valid. On a typical noisy orientation day, when the ladies were getting their showers done, Latesha went off on another girl in the dorm. She grabbed the inmate by the hair, pulled her out of her chair onto the tiled floor, and repeatedly smashed the back of her head onto the floor. The girl soon lost consciousness, but Latesha wasn't done. While another inmate hit the emergency button to call for security staff, Latesha dragged the girl by the hair, still unconscious, into a bathroom stall and forced her face underwater into a toilet. At this time, staff entered the bathroom and pulled Latesha off of the other inmate. The victim had no serious injuries from the brutal assault. During the investigative interviews, there was no reason found for the attack by Latesha, and she wasn't offering a reason. At one point, she said, "I didn't like her face," but that was as far as the investigation went. Latesha was placed in SMU housing for the protection of the other inmates around her.

I tried to find out some history on her to give some light as to why she was so hateful and violent. She came from a long line of abusive relationships that started at a very young age. That was no surprise. She was born addicted to meth from an alcoholic mother who couldn't care for her. She was doing drugs at age eight, was a heavy drinker, and was in and out of foster homes before the ink on all the transfers was dry.

It took a lot of convincing to get her to agree to see the psych doctor. Once she did agree to see her, it took a great deal of work to develop a sense of trust and a good repertoire with the psychiatrist. It took many visits with the doctor to get Latesha to agree to take medications for her severe mental illness. But as expected, she wouldn't show up at medline and didn't take them faithfully so the drugs could help her. Then she refused all medications and refused to see psych at all anymore. We were back to square one.

Some days, Latesha would be observed laughing when no one was around or shouting angrily at someone who wasn't there. It was minute to minute and day by day, and everyone wondered when she would become violent and out of control again. Everyone, inmates and staff alike, knew to step carefully and speak softly around her.

MARTHA

Martha, an inmate well over three hundred pounds, continued to gain weight without reasonable cause. She had been working for property and commissary, handing out clothing and food items ordered by inmates. Her supervisor reported that her behavior was good, and she didn't have any concerns. At the end of every shift, the inmates are given a pat-down by a female officer to make sure nothing was being taken by the inmate. Keeping in mind that Martha was very obese, the property officer did her usual pat-down and sent the inmate to her housing unit. The officer working in Martha's housing unit randomly selected Martha for an unclothed search upon her return from her work assignment. Once Martha removed all her clothing and turned around, nothing seemed out of the ordinary. That was, until the officer told her to lift up her large breasts. The inmate complied. It was then that the jig was up. Two Snickers bars fell to the floor. She was ordered to lift up her upper large tummy roll. Three more Snickers landed at Martha's feet. When she was finally ordered to lift up her lower belly roll, Mr. Goodbar and Baby Ruth joined the Snickers on the floor. As the officer stared in disbelief, the inmate could only say, "Damn. There went my midnight snack."

We see a lot of inmates who come into prison with drug problems. Many of those will tell you that they don't have a problem with drugs—they just got caught. But one thing we hear all the time is no matter why an inmate comes to prison, it's never their fault. It's inevitably someone else's fault.

ZOEY

Zoey was a happy, well-adjusted girl and lived with her parents in a quiet little town in Colorado. She was daddy's girl, and the two were inseparable. Zoey's mom, Carol, cared more about her booze than either one of them. When Zoey was eight, her parents divorced. Soon after the breakup, Zoey's father took a job promotion that included a relocation across the country. It broke Zoey's heart the day he said goodbye.

It wasn't long before Carol married Gary, one of the drunks Carol dated from the bar she spent her time at. Zoey disliked Gary the moment she first met him. He was always touching her and putting her on his lap. Carol and Gary were drunk most of the time, so Zoey stayed in her room.

One night after Carol had passed out on the couch, Gary came into Zoey's room. He climbed into the sleeping little girl's bed and began touching her. He put his hand over her mouth, silencing her. He told her if she ever said a word about this, he would kill her father. Zoey cried quietly while he raped her. Gary's visits to her room continued until Zoey was fifteen years old. On a cold November night, she waited until she knew her mother and stepfather were asleep. She grabbed her coat, her mittens, her backpack (filled with six cans of tuna), and her clothes. She climbed out her bedroom window and ran as fast as she could. Zoey hitchhiked her way to Las Vegas. Once her babysitting money was spent, she walked the streets trying to figure out where she would get her next meal and where she would sleep.

A Mexican man about fifty years old with a kind face and torn clothes approached her and offered to help her out. He said his name was Ezra, and he had been where she was now and sensed she could use a helping hand. She was desperate and couldn't refuse. He took her to an underground water runoff tunnel. It was wet and dark and smelled damp and dirty. He handed her a flashlight and told her to follow him. He took her to a little shack made of pieces of wood, cloth, and cardboard. Inside was a pillow and a blanket on a bed of branches and foam. Ezra told her she could stay there for now until they could make her a place of her own. He opened a can of beans for her to eat. Even cold, the beans were like heaven, and she gobbled them down. She laid down and slept soundly. In the morning when she awoke, Ezra handed her a cup of hot coffee in a tin cup. She changed her clothes and went looking for a job. After a week, she still hadn't found anyone who would hire her. She met a girl, Marilyn, who said she was twenty-one but looked much younger. She said she could hook her up to make some cash. Zoey jumped at the offer. The job would be working the strip as a prostitute. At this point, she felt there were no other options and took the job. Her first client was a nicely dressed man in his fifties. Zoey was terrified but did what she had to. Afterward, the man paid her fifty dollars, and Zoey worked to convince herself that it was worth it. She bought some food and coffee and returned to her little shack in the tunnel. Later that evening, she met up with Ezra and went farther into the tunnel, where several others were gathered around a bonfire. They were doing all kinds of drugs. Ezra handed her a rolled marijuana cigarette and convinced her to take a drag, promising her it would take the edge off. She had never tried drugs in her life but found the marijuana made her relaxed and worry free. Meeting at the bonfire became a nightly event. In a short time, Zoey found meth to be her favorite release. She required more and more and needed the drug just to function. She became thinner and thinner. She had sores over her face, arms, and chest. This began to affect her job income because johns weren't interested in having sex with someone covered with sores. She needed money to pay for the meth. She began stealing more and became reckless.

One night, the robbery of a local businessman's home went wrong. The silent alarm was tripped and Zoey didn't make it out in time and was arrested. She already had an arrest list as long as her arm for prostitution and petty theft. Zoey went to jail. When she finally went to court, she ended up with a judge who had had enough meetings with Zoey. She was sentenced to two years in prison.

Zoey was the first inmate I'd ever met who said she was so happy to be in prison. She had a warm bed, guaranteed three hot meals a day, books to read, and activities like volleyball, basketball, and card games to keep her entertained. She gained weight back, and her skin sores healed. She knew she'd probably always crave meth, but through alcohol and drug treatment, she was learning ways to deal with those cravings.

Zoey quickly came out of her shell during her incarceration. She took part in every opportunity available. She maintained excellent behavior and avoided all gang advances trying to get her to join up. She avoided relationships and remained a loner. She told me it was better that way because then there was no chance of loss. She knew loss very well. When she ran away, she lost contact with her father. Despite trying to move heaven and earth to find her dad, she never did find him. It was as if he had disappeared. She still missed him and never wanted to go through that again with someone else.

Zoey contacted her mother only once, to try to find her father. Carol was drunk and incoherent on the phone when Zoey called her. Zoey never brought charges against her stepfather despite encouragement to do so. She said she couldn't go through all those horrible memories again even though she could put him behind bars for a very long time. She vowed to never speak to her mother again and wrote her and her rapist husband out of her life for good. She said she would never forget the years of sexual abuse, and despite all she'd learned about forgiveness, she doubted she would ever forgive her stepfather.

Zoey enrolled in the welding program, and by the time of her release from the women's prison, she had attained her welding certificate. This achievement gained her a welding job waiting for her once she was released. She also had a home at a women's halfway house as well.

She promised me at her medical discharge physical that she had come too far to ever let meth back into her life ever again because she remembered all too well how it had taken over and destroyed her life. When she walked out of the prison doors, I'll never forget her big smile and the look of pure hope for a new and better life.

I hope she made it.

TINA AND SHEENA

On a hot Tuesday in July, Tina came back to the facility for her fourth time on a drug charge. She was angry and blamed the world around her. A routine admission question we ask is, what brought the woman to prison, and how long is her sentence? To these questions, Tina replied, "I didn't do anything wrong. It's not my fault that stupid judge sent me here!" The truth was that Tina had sold a large amount of meth, marijuana, and Percocet to an undercover agent in the parking lot of a grade school. She went on to say, "The cops just got it in for me, that's all!"

Sheena came to prison in the van from county jail that day with Tina. Both women had been in our custody multiple times—frequent flyers, if you will. Both were booked in and fingerprinted, and with every inmate's arrival, a urine analysis is done immediately to test for illicit drugs, pregnancy, and venereal infections (STDs). Sheena passed her urine drug screen with flying colors. That in itself was a surprise given her history. Sheena did not appear to be guilty of anything when one looked at her. She was a very quiet, petite young girl with long blonde hair and a sweet face. She looked no more than fifteen years old.

It was only a day or so before the complaints started coming to staff's attention that there was meth in the new arrival orientation dorm. Perhaps it wasn't being shared with everyone, and someone got mad. Who knows? The process required another drug screen on every inmate in orientation. Several inmates, including Sheena and Tina, came up positive for meth. The next step was an unclothed search by a female officer. The officer never touches the inmate during an unclothed search, but the inmate has to flip their hair over and toss it around, show the armpits, lift the breasts, and ultimately do the "squat and cough." Body cavity searches were not allowed at the prison, so it was well-known that many times we were unable to find out which inmate had physically brought the drugs into the facility. Women would insert baggies of drugs as well as prescription bottles into their vaginas for later consumption, so often the searches proved uneventful. Then it was Sheena's turn for the strip search. Unfortunately for her, when Sheena squatted and coughed for the officer, a small, clear baggie with a white powdery substance fell onto the floor. Soon after, testing showed the substance to be methamphetamine. During inmate questioning and testimony, it was reported that inmates would "find" the meth on top of the toilet paper dispenser under packaged panty liners. Whoever found it, used it. For these women with so many addiction issues, the temptation was too great and preceded thoughts about the consequences and how the drug came into the prison.

Bringing drugs into a correctional facility is a very serious thing. The inmate is officially charged with this crime and the highest level of write-up issued within the prison walls. Then the consequences start. This may include being locked down in solitary confinement for several days with no commissary (snacks, etc.), no phone use, and no family visits, as well as many other losses of privileges.

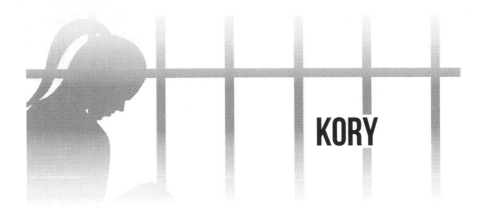

KORY

Kory had a rough start in life like so many of the women in prison. By the age of eighteen, she had her first child. She didn't know who Chandler's father was. When she partied, she partied hard. Having sex with multiple men was a common occurrence. Kory was heavily addicted to hardcore drugs. She lived in a rundown apartment on the south side of town with her fourteen-month-old son; her boyfriend, TJ; and three of his buddies. She was able to keep a job working at a cheap hotel cleaning rooms. Every two weeks when Kory got her paycheck, buying drugs was her number one expense. Food for her son and rent expenses were last, if there was even any money left. TJ worked at a truck stop changing oil and tires for the customers who came through. Like Kory, getting high was his priority in life.

The night the nightmare began, TJ had come into a large amount of meth from his dealer, Matty. Matty warned TJ to not use as much as usual because the stuff was laced with fentanyl and was a guaranteed "higher than high." The three roommates were out at a house party, so it was just TJ, Kory, and baby Chandler. TJ put a tourniquet on his upper arm, injected the liquid gold into a blood vessel, and handed the syringe to Kory. She followed suit and emptied the meth into her body. The room began to spin.

Chandler kept crying; he was likely hungry. TJ was yelling at Kory to shut her kid up, or he'd do it. Kory told him to just ignore it, but Chandler wouldn't stop screaming. TJ was furious. He grabbed the boy's arm and jerked him around, breaking Chandler's arm. As the child continued to scream, TJ became angrier. He started punching the boy's face over and over. Kory simply sat on the couch and watched this take place right in front of her. She didn't get up and try to stop the violent attack on her son. She didn't beg him to stop. She sat there and watched. TJ then threw the child. The baby's head hit the wall. Chandler stopped crying. He never cried again. Kory watched her boyfriend kill her baby boy and did nothing to stop it. Nothing at all.

Kory was sentenced to twenty-five years without the possibility of parole. When she arrived at the prison, I did her admission medical exam. She was an angry young woman. Her answers to my entrance questions were short and curt. She said, "I'm sick of this bullshit! Why do I have to answer all these fuckin' questions?" I told her she could act appropriately and complete the entrance questions, or she could sit locked in an infirmary cell until she was ready to complete the process. She grabbed my paperwork and threw it across the room, yelling, "Fuck your paperwork, and fuck you!" I radioed Captain Zina and requested immediate assistance. She responded with another CO in less than two minutes to find the inmate in a rage, throwing everything she could get her hands on in the infirmary. She ordered the inmate to stop, face the wall, and cuff up. Kory took a fight stance with feet spread and fists up and stated, "Make me, you fucking cunt!" Captain Zina and CO Robert quickly obtained control and handcuffed her wrists. The captain said she was going to give Kory an hour or so to cool down and perhaps continue the admission process later when she's ready to be compliant. The captain and CO Robert decided to hang around for a while. Kory was screaming profanities nonstop. Within a couple minutes, we heard a banging sound coming from Kory's cell. The captain looked through the cell door window. Kory was slamming her forehead against the wall with all the pent-up fury she had within her. There was blood on the wall and a hole in the sheet rock. Blood was running down her face. The captain quickly unlocked the cell, and she and Robert subdued her. Zina then radioed for more security staff. Within one minute, three more COs were there. Zina told CO Heather to obtain the restraint chair. The captain continued to hold down Kory's arms while Robert and the other two COs assisted in securing the inmate. Zina kept trying to gain compliance by talking to Kory in an attempt to calm her and get her to settle down. But Kory had no intention to comply and continued fighting the officers. Blood ran into her eyes. I asked her if she would let me clean and dress the wound on her forehead. She told me to fucking go to hell. Okay, no medical assistance will be taking place at this time. Heather arrived with the restraint chair. Captain again asked Kory if she would comply. Kory spat in Zina's face. A spit hood was secured over Kory's face and secured loosely around her throat.

The team placed her in the restraint chair and secured Velcro straps from the chair around her forehead, shoulders, arms, wrists, waist, thighs, and ankles. It was my job to assess her to assure that the straps were not too tight and cutting off blood supply. Security staff had to be posted near her constantly while she was in the restraint chair. The CO would release one limb at a time and try to do range of motion exercises with her. She continuously fought the CO and refused to do the exercises. The warden was notified, as was usual with any restraints used on an inmate.

Physical restraints such as a restraint chair or a restraint mattress can have dangerous effects on an inmate over time. This is especially significant if the inmate continues to fight against the restraints. The muscles start to produce lactic acid, and this process could lead to asphyxia (inability to breathe) and eventually death. Therefore, constant observation and precautions must be taken. This includes releasing one limb at a time. The CO tries to do range of motion (ROM) exercises with the inmate, and if the inmate is still fighting, they aren't very successful. If the inmate tries to kick or hit the CO, this is very similar to ROM, but the fighting inmate doesn't know that! In addition, nurses are nearby and also check to assure that the restraints aren't too tight and the nurse can easily slip two fingers within the straps. They also check the fingers and toes for good blood flow, ask the inmate to wiggle their fingers and toes, and ask if she has any pain.

In Kory's case, she told me to fuck off. Yup, she's able to talk just fine. My mission was completed.

She fought for hours and refused to cooperate at all. I notified the physician, who ordered the cocktail. This included two syringes with three drugs to calm her down before the lactic acid buildup put her at serious risk. An oral form of the drugs had to first be offered to Kory. She again told me to go fuck myself. Next, I drew up the drugs in muscle injection form. I had another nurse assist me. We injected both arms simultaneously. As I observed Kory over the next hour, the drugs had no effect on her. She was still at a dangerous level of rage. I called the doctor again, and the cocktail was repeated. In about one and a half hours, Captain Zina asked Kory if she would calm down and be taken out of the chair and put in a call, where she could lie down. The security team of five staff, fully dressed in forced cell garb, released her hands from the chair and applied handcuffs. Kory's Velcro straps were released, and the team placed her in a solitary confinement cell. The staff then backed out of the cell and locked and secured the door.

Kory was on continuous camera observation by security staff in the Control booth with ten- to fifteen-minute physical checks by security staff. Once she had calmed down, the physical exhaustion hit her like a truck. She refused most meals, telling the staff to leave her alone. She slept for the greater part of the next forty-eight hours.

Once Kory regained her strength, her bad behaviors returned as well. Kory emptied the toilet paper roll, shoved it all into her toilet, and flooded her cell. Captain Shane asked her repeatedly if she would comply to be moved to another cell so hers could be mopped and cleaned. Her response was, "Fuck you. Come on and fight me, bitches. I'm going to kill your asses!" The team was once again assembled, and they stormed her cell. Restraints were applied while she kicked, swung her fists, and screamed profanities the entire time.

Kory's bad behavior continued throughout the next thirty days of disciplinary detention (DD). The team of case managers, medical, and security captains met weekly. It was decided that Kory would be released to the medium- to maximum-security floor and housed in a single-bed cell with restrictions. She would have to earn privileges with good behavior.

Two days after her release to the floor, she assaulted CO Michael because he wouldn't buy her a bottle of soda. Kory punched Michael in the shoulder and kicked him in the shin. He then called for assistance over the radio. Four staff responded within one minute. Kory was pushed face forward against the wall. The staff cuffed her hands behind her back and placed her back in a DD cell. She wouldn't comply to place her hands in the slot for cuff removal, which would have been a benefit for her. Her thinking was completely irrational. She presented with the same strength and rage as before.

The team of case managers, security captains, medical services director, and the warden resumed weekly meetings to evaluate Kory's behavior for the last week and determine whether at least one restriction could be lifted. It was decided that she could have crayons and coloring pages. If she shredded the paper, flooded her cell, or showed bad behaviors again, her regards would go back to ground zero. This chain of events would go on until her release from prison one year later. Despite all the counseling, appointments with her psychiatrist, case manager, and medications, Kory showed little improvement with her behavior and mental status by the day she left the facility.

Three months later, Kory died from a heroin overdose. She was found deceased in her car at a parking lot. The needle was still in her arm.

SARAH

Sarah had been in and out of prison most of her adult life. Although she looked like about sixty years old, she was only thirty-seven. Many years of hard drinking and drugging had left her looking like a sick old lady with thin tangled gray hair and wrinkles across her face. On some Sunday afternoons, her boyfriend would come to visit. At that time, the chairs and tables in the visitation room were standard height. Now, all the tables are small tables no taller than the seat of the chairs beside them, and for good reason.

One Sunday, I received a call that Sarah had returned from visitation, and there seemed to be something wrong with her. She seemed "out of it," as the officer stated on the phone. I advised the officer to send her over to the infirmary, and I would check her out. The officer called back a short time later and told me that the inmate couldn't walk. Two officers assisted Sarah into a wheelchair and brought her to the medical department. At first glance, I could tell that something wasn't quite right. Her speech was slower than normal, and so were her upper body movements. The captain and I decided that we needed to obtain a urine specimen from her to test for drugs. Sarah insisted that she could not pee, so we waited. And waited. And waited. We finally decided to place a "hat," a urine collection device, on the toilet. Sarah would not, or could not, stand. The captain and I lifted her out of the wheelchair and placed her on the toilet. I noticed something out of the corner of my eye and motioned to the floor beside the toilet to the captain. There on the floor, next to the toilet, was a white pill that had not been there before. Sarah seemed to become more tired and continued to state she could not provide a urine specimen, so I decided to call the doctor. I reported the scenario to the physician. He agreed with my thoughts on this situation and gave me an order to assess for bladder distention and catheterize if indicated. The captain and I lifted Sarah back into the wheelchair and moved her to the exam table for assessment.

As I performed a nursing assessment on Sarah, it was clear that her bladder appeared to be very full and distended. After calling the physician for an order to proceed, I placed a foley catheter (a thin tube) up into her bladder and obtained hundreds of milliliters of urine. She adamantly did not want us to test her urine. But that was not the end of this scenario. During the catheterization procedure, clear plastic wrap and more white pills appeared on the paper-covered exam table. It was later found during the investigation that while at visitation with Sarah's boyfriend, camera footage showed the boyfriend had passed her a small package from beneath the table. During a small ruckus with other visiting children in the visitation room, Sarah appeared to put the package inside her vagina. Unfortunately for Sarah, not long after visitation ended, her package had managed to unwrap itself, and her body was absorbing large quantities of Percocet, a narcotic. Sarah could have died from a drug overdose that day.

Now we know why everyone in visitation sits at kiddie tables: because it's much harder to pass little packages under them.

TULSA

With a hot cup of coffee, I eased into the chair at my desk while mentally preparing myself to tackle the piles of paperwork in front of me. About five minutes later, I heard yelling coming from down the hall from my office. I stepped into the hall and saw a familiar face struggling against the two officers who were assisting her to the booking room. I returned to my office and whispered, "Here we go again."

Tulsa was strip-searched and fingerprinted, and she completed the interview process as she had several times before in her twenty-four years of life. She was back in prison on drug charges. Her history with drug use went back to the age of nine, when her own mother would shoot her up with heroin and lock her in her bedroom. Tulsa's mother, Katt, partied hard and had lots of men coming and going from their house each night. There was a coffee table with almost every kind of drug one could imagine, and lots of booze. For drugs or money, Katt would allow the men to take turns entertaining themselves with her nine-year-old daughter in the bedroom. This horrifying lifestyle went on until Tulsa ran away from home at the age of twelve.

With no money and no place to go, it was only a matter of time before she fell into the hands of what seemed at the time to be a very nice man. She was hungry, cold, and scared, so his offer to do her a favor and help her felt like God was finally answering her prayers. He put her up in a cheap hotel with a warm bed. Tulsa savored the hot shower and felt the hot water wash away her cares. She crawled into the bed and wrapped the faded olive green comforter tightly around her thin, ninety-five-pound body. For the first time in years, she felt warm and safe.

Suddenly, the blankets were ripped from her body. The lights were blinding. Gary, the nice man who had just helped her out hours before, stood over her body, laughing, shouting, and reeking of alcohol. He grabbed her arm and started tearing at her clothes. There were other men standing around the bed laughing and shouting, "Give it to her, Gary! Show her who's boss!" Gary raped her. She lost track of how many other men violated her too. Before she mentally shut down as she had learned years ago, she thought to herself, "I ran right into what I ran away from."

Tulsa decided to prostitute for Gary at the hotel. She felt too tired to fight it and resigned herself to this lifestyle as all there was for her. Besides, she had a roof over her head and all the drugs she wanted to "numb out." Getting busted by the cops for drugs or prostitution was more of an annoyance than a big deal. On a blustery, cold Tuesday night, customers were pretty thin, so Gary told her he needed her to help with a drug drop-off. No big deal, she thought—until she took the cash and handed the large suitcase full of meth over to an undercover DEA agent. Game over.

PEARL

We were never able to make Pearl feel well. No matter what we tried, her ongoing "vaginal infection" complaints continued to recur. Although symptoms and testing for bacterial and yeast infections continued to be negative, she insisted she needed treatment. We ended up treating her with different creams and pills in the hopes that something would help, or at least stop the incessant complaining and demands for repeated vaginal exams. Nothing worked. We got to a point where we would limit her vaginal exams to once each month. So Pearl started sending us panty liners through the in-house mail to "prove" she has a discharge problem. She was written up for this unsafe and unsanitary behavior. On one exam day, she was taken into the medical exam room and asked to disrobe from the waist down, put on the gown, and sit down on the exam table—a routine with which she was all too familiar. When the physician and the nurse entered the exam room to perform the assessment, Pearl was standing stark naked with her arm outstretched toward both medical staff faces holding a wad of tissues in her hand. She said, "See? See? I wiped the discharge from my vagina to show you! Smell it! I told you I have bad discharge!" Pearl was directed to dispose of the tissues in the bio-hazard garbage and immediately put on the gown provided for her.

As time went on, we decided that Pearl's complaining over something that didn't exist needed to stop. So Pearl grievanced us. This is a process that occurs when an inmate feels wronged by prison staff or prison rules. The warden and I sat down with Pearl one day to discuss her concerns and hopefully find an answer that would meet her needs. She went on and on about her suffering, saying, "Warden, it's awful! It smells just terrible down there. And it's gotten worse! After I take a shower, my feet even stink!" No, I did not bust out laughing, but it was very difficult not to. Instead, I calmly asked her how that could happen. She told me that when the water ran down, it picked up the bad vaginal smell, and it stuck to her feet. (I was still not laughing. Amazing.) I quietly asked her if she used soap, and she said she did. I told her that I learned in a science class years ago that when you use soap and water during bathing, the soap attaches to the dirt/soil and carries it down the drain. I told her that if there is any soil or odor, it does not jump off the soap and attach itself to her feet. To this, she said, "Really? I didn't know that!" Oh, my.

Pearl was difficult in a lot of ways. She frequently demanded attention. When she didn't get the attention she wanted, good or bad, she would assault staff. One afternoon after she was seen by the provider, a CO came to collect her from an infirmary holding cell and escort her back to her own solitary cell in the SMU. The officer asked her to stand. Apparently, Pearl had other ideas. She began screaming profanities at the CO and refused to comply. When the security officer approached Pearl to assist her to her feet, she kicked the officer in the stomach as hard as she could, sending the CO backward across the room and slamming her back into the wall. The officer was five months pregnant. Another CO stormed into the cell and quickly obtained control over the inmate. She was "cuffed and stuffed" before she knew what happened.

The CO who was kicked in the belly was immediately sent to her OB doctor for an assessment. Luckily, both mom and baby were going to be okay.

Staff learned a valuable lesson that day. Never let your guard down, always expect the unexpected, and never try to handle a potentially violent inmate like Pearl alone.

SHARON

We received a phone call from the industries director stating that her sewing department supervisor and multiple inmates were complaining that there was something wrong with Sharon, an elderly inmate with a very long sentence.

They reported that a horrible smell was coming from her work station, where she sewed T-shirts. They requested that she have a medical assessment because something was truly wrong with her. Sharon did have a pelvic exam in the past where a large amount of stool was present in her vaginal area. We suspected that this had happened again.

The physician met with her in the exam room and then called me in as well. She filled me in about the complaint and said she did not notice an odor of any kind. I didn't notice any odor either. As I visited with Sharon, I told her that sometimes inmates make these things up just to pick on other inmates. She said she was shocked and wanted to know who said these things about her. She felt humiliated and embarrassed. We told her not to worry about it and to go back to work as if nothing had happened. I thought forgetting about it wouldn't be a problem for her because Sharon had been showing signs of dementia. Still, I checked into this foul odor complaint.

Inmates are allowed to order frozen foods, but there is limited storage to keep them frozen. It turns out that Sharon ordered two large bags of cauliflower and broccoli. She had no freezer storage, so she ate all four bags of the vegetables in one day. Sharon had a very severe case of flatulence, or gas, and was farting a great deal at her sewing station. Odor problem found.

Later that same day, Sharon was put on suicide watch. Her level of embarrassment was devastating for her, but was she truly suicidal? Probably not, but we have to take seriously every inmate with suicidal ideation. After a night alone under suicide watch, she composed herself, declared no suicidal thoughts, and went back to work.

When Sharon first arrived at the prison, staff and inmates felt a little sorry for her. She was an elderly, somewhat frail appearing woman, who was soft-spoken and showed signs of dementia. It was so hard to accept that this little old lady was capable of the crime she had committed that had landed her in prison for the rest of her life. Some four or so years ago, Sharon began poisoning her husband with rat poison in his food. He became ill but wasn't dying as Sharon had planned, so she decided to take a more drastic measure. While her husband sat on the toilet, completely unaware of what was about to happen, Sharon was preparing to finish what she had started. She grabbed him and quickly tied his hands together with duct tape so he could not free his hands. Then she placed the plastic bag over his head and secured it around and around his face and neck multiple times so he could not breathe. While he tried to cry out for help, each breath sucking the plastic further into his mouth, Sharon stepped back out of his reach and waited. She was not filled with emotions of any kind while she watched him struggle to live. She felt only the calm of a job completed as she stared at his blue, distorted face and watched him become limp. The beginning of the end.

This unthinkable crime just didn't seem to fit the thin, gray-haired woman dressed in an orange jumpsuit with shackles and chains standing before me.

I had just entered the prison at eight in the morning and was in the process of signing in, planning for a day filled with the pile of paperwork on my desk. Suddenly, a medical emergency was called overhead and on my radio. I dropped my coat and went running down the stairs to the honor dorm in the medium- to maximum-custody unit. It was Sharon. Security staff had pulled the blankets off of her to reveal a bed filled with blood and Sharon lying in it. The officer reported to me that she was unable to wake Sharon to report for work in the industries unit. Sharon had taken a razor blade and cut her right wrist very deeply, through tendons and muscle to the wrist bones. She had planned this very carefully so there would be no blood seen anywhere while she worked to complete her suicide attempt.

Earlier the evening before, Sharon had called her daughter on the telephone; all phone calls to and from inmates are recorded for security purposes. Her daughter was still grieving due to her mother's murder of her father. The daughter had said hurtful things to Sharon and told her she was exactly where she belonged, that she deserved all she got, and that she never wanted to see her mother ever again. Sharon went to her room and prepared for what she was about to do. When her dorm mates all left and went to the IDR for supper, she placed three cotton and plastic puppy pads on top of plastic garbage bags on her bed. She placed her extra blankets under her right arm for absorbency. She placed a tall quart glass in a large gallon-size popcorn bowl. Then she hid everything with her bedspread until it was time for lights out. Once all the ladies in her dorm were asleep, Sharon initiated her plan. She had stolen a tourniquet from the infirmary during doctor call with the physician's assistant and tied it very tightly around her right arm. Then she carved deeper and deeper a gash in her right wrist. She positioned her wrist over the plastic quart glass and let the blood fill the glass. Every time an officer walked through the dorm to perform an hourly well-being check on each inmate, Sharon had her reading lamp on, and she pretended to be reading a book all through the night. Any time her wrist would begin to clot and the bleeding would slow down, she would just cut into the wound to keep the blood flowing. Once the drinking glass was full, it would overflow into the large bowl. When the bowl was full, it would run over and soak slowly into all the folded blankets and pads.

When I got to Sharon's bedside, she was as white as her sheet once was, and the officer was performing chest compressions. I told her to stop and checked for a pulse. No pulse. We resumed CPR. I wrapped her clotted wrist with a dressing. The nurse on duty handed me the stethoscope. There was no breathing or heartbeat. We put a face mask on her and turned up the oxygen. The ambulance was on the way. I put an IV in her foot because there was so much activity going on with her upper body, and I opened the IV fluids up as fast as it would go. Some staff were performing CPR while others were removing the containers overflowing with blood and the blood-soaked items around her. We stopped CPR, and still there was no pulse or breathing. We placed the defibrillator pads on her chest and shocked her but did not get a pulse. Sharon didn't have enough blood for her heart to beat; this was similar to a car with no gas in the tank. The paramedics arrived. I gave them a quick report of everything we knew and the times of what we had done since we found her. The paramedics connected her to a heart monitor and started an intraosseous IV, an IV needle placed down into the bone, into her shin because they could not find a vein. We ran the fluids into her body as fast as we could. We got a pulse, and she began breathing. She was later flown to another hospital ICU, where she was stabilized. She had reconstructive surgery to her badly damaged wrist and was seen by psychiatry for her mental health.

Sharon doesn't remember much of the events. That's probably for the best. She and her daughter repaired their relationship, and she is happy the prison staff saved her life.

NEVAEA

Nevaea was born in a small village in Africa. She had two brothers and was the only girl in her family. At the age of nine years old, Nevaea watched the political unrest in her country become a full-blown war that invaded her village. Truckloads of men armed with guns arrived and began shooting and killing men, women, and children. Men rushed into her home. She watched them shoot her father and her mother. She saw the blood pouring out of their bodies and pooling on the dirt floor. She was terrified and could not move, much less think of running for her life. One of the men grabbed the front of her dress, picked her up off the floor, and laughed before he punched her in her face. He dropped her onto the dirt floor, unzipped his pants, and raped her. Then everything went black.

Several years later, at the age of twenty-three, she came to America with nothing but the clothes on her back and her aunt by her side. Aunt Mesha was the only known family member who had survived the war. The memories of the massacre also followed her and haunted her daily.

Nevaea carried a deep rage inside her. One day while walking the aisles of the grocery market, she heard three teenage girls laughing at her and calling her names. "Black trash, stupid nigger." Her anger boiled up inside her. She left the store and sat in her car. As she sat behind the wheel, her anger escalated. When she saw the three girls leave the store and walk down the street, she started her car and began following them. She then pressed the pedal to the floor, swerved the car to the right, and drove over two of the girls, leaving them badly injured and bleeding in the street.

It didn't take long until she was arrested and sentenced to prison. She felt she had been wronged and didn't belong in prison, because they had deserved it.

Nevaea didn't make any friends in prison as most female inmates usually do. She remained quiet and solitary. Every time she broke a rule or got in a fight, she'd scream that all the staff were racist and picking on her. She never took accountability for her actions that got her into trouble, and she played the racist card frequently.

Her post-traumatic stress syndrome (PTSD) was severe. She had episodes of nonresponsiveness and convulsions. She would then be taken to the infirmary and given an injection to calm her down. After multiple medical tests and a visit with the neurologist, no conclusive diagnosis could be confirmed. It was suspected that she had been faking the episodes to get away from other inmates, get calming medications, and sleep in a nice, quiet cell with room service and attentive nursing care. One day during another seizure-type episode and nonresponsiveness, it was verbally said to her that she would not be getting any medications whatsoever and no room service. She was soon wide awake with no symptoms, and she asked to go back to her cell. That was the last episode she had during the rest of her incarceration.

SUMMER

This inmate didn't stand much of a chance before she was even born.

Summer was born at the state hospital for the mentally ill. Medical records show that a male sex offender at the state hospital had raped a mentally ill and incapacitated woman who resided at the hospital. Nine months later, Summer was born.

Summer spent most of her life in and out of the state hospital for mental illness. She was placed in many foster homes over years. Each family sent her back into child protective services due to her behavior: acting out, running away, destruction of their property, and criminal activity. She was well-known by the staff at the jail and juvenile hall.

On a blustery cold day in January, the county sheriff's department brought in Summer handcuffed and in leg irons. After the corrections officers booked her and provided her with the necessities to serve the beginning of her two-year drug possession charge, she came to medical for her initial assessment. She had just turned eighteen years old.

Summer sat quietly in a chair in the corner of the room. She was a chubby native woman with short black hair who presented with her head down throughout the interview. She spoke only when she had to and answered my questions with a one- or two-word response and with a flat affect. She wore large, round glasses and would not make eye contact. She had new and old track marks down both arms from IV drug use, but that wasn't a surprise to me at all. What was shocking was the fact that her arms were covered from shoulders to wrists with scars from cutting herself. A strip search showed cutting marks down her thighs as well.

Cuts seen on female inmates are caused from one or two things, or a combination of the two. Scars from cut wrists may have been the source of a failed suicide attempt. I soon learned that the scars on this woman in front of me didn't look like attempted suicide. Summer was someone who would be labeled as a cutter. Cutting is when someone suffers from mental or emotional pain and chooses to replace this emotional pain with physical pain. These women have said that the physical pain is easier to live with.

In cases like this, where there may be concern, an initial mental health appraisal is completed by behavioral health staff to see where the inmate is at. Summer expressed suicidal thoughts throughout the interview. It was decided that she would be placed under observation for her safety. She was placed on an initial low level of observation in the orientation unit. All new arrivals live in a segregated community for the first thirty days.

Two days later, it was decided to lift observation status as Karen seemed stable. Five days after Summer's arrival, she attempted to hang herself in the orientation dorm while the other inmates were in the library. Luckily, staff found her quickly. She was placed back on observation with frequent staff contacts.

On day twelve, Summer tried for the attention of another inmate. When she didn't receive that attention, she began picking up all the chairs in the one-room dorm and throwing them.

Not long after this, Summer was placed on observation a third time for suicidal thoughts. She began picking at her arm until she broke the skin, causing her arm to drip with blood. She was asked multiple times to stop, but she refused. This resulted in her placement in the restraint chair, causing full immobility. Nursing had to check the color and movement of all four extremities. Her wound was tended to and dressed. When asked why she was tearing at the flesh in her arm, Summer stated, "Because it feels good." When she finally agreed to stop self-harming, she was released from the restraint chair and placed in an observation cell with a camera. Within seventy-two hours, Summer had ripped open the wound in her arm and began smearing her blood all over the windows and walls. She was hepatitis C positive. This resulted in her placement in the restraint chair again.

Less than one month from her arrival, while living in general population, Summer told staff that she had ingested an entire bottle of aspirin and melatonin. She was immediately taken to the ER. The toxicology results show no levels of either drug in her system. On her return to the prison, she was placed on suicide watch for the fourth time.

It wasn't long while on observation before she used a paper spoon to cut open her arm wound again. She told staff that she would never stop harming herself, so staff would have to enter her cell and remove her again and again. Summer was placed back in the restraint chair.

After she agreed to not cut anymore, she was moved to the observation cell. With an order for only finger foods and no utensils of any kind, Summer used the cardboard from inside her toilet paper roll to cut at her arm. Nursing again entered the cell and bandaged her arm.

Later that day, Summer took the bandage from her arm, climbed up onto the sink, and put the bandage over the camera. She then used wet toilet paper to cover all the windows to her cell so staff could not see her. When the officers opened her cell to uncover the windows and camera, Summer assumed an aggressive stance and was ready to fight. Staff used OC spray (pepper spray) on her to get her to back down.

On Summer's sixth week in prison, she attempted to hang herself with a ripped-up sheet. When staff intervened and cut her down, she was angry that she was not allowed to die. She was placed on observation a fifth time.

One week after the hanging attempt, she broke her eye glasses and used the glass to cut open her arm. There was blood all over the floor, and Summer was pumping her fist in an attempt to cause more blood to spill to the floor. Staff slipped and slid in the blood while trying to control the bleeding from her arm.

Three days later, Summer was cuffed and shackled to attend a phone call with her attorney. As staff tried to remove her cuffs, she resisted and punched a female officer in the face, resulting in OC spray being used on her again.

The frequent attempts at self-harm and assaults on staff continued in the following weeks. Summer ripped the television off of the wall when allowed day room time to watch TV. When a nurse was trying to give her the evening medications through the food port to her cell, Summer grabbed the medication card and quickly popped all of the Seroquel out of the blister pack and quickly swallowed them all. Summer was again taken to the ER to have her stomach pumped. She was hospitalized under twenty-four-hour supervision for three days.

Upon her return to her cell at the prison, it didn't take long before she removed the compression wrap the hospital had put around her arm and attempted to use it to hang herself from her sink. Staff had to use a cut-down tool to get it off from around her neck.

The state hospital was contacted again and again, requesting admission for this mentally ill woman. They repeatedly denied the request, stating, "She is very behavioral," as the reason why.

Summer continued to spiral deeper and deeper. She began refusing to drink any water, believing staff had poisoned it because one morning, she stated she felt dizzy after drinking it. She tried to drown herself in her toilet twice.

Upon receiving the sanctions or discipline for her write-ups, she became very angry, stood on her sink, and tried to choke herself with her suicide smock (a very heavy garment used for protection and warmth for a suicidal inmate). She later stated that she'd hoped she'd pass out, fall onto the floor, and break her neck.

The very next day, Summer was observed to have reopened her arm wound and was pulling out pieces of flesh and throwing them on the floor. That night, Summer covered her windows and camera again with toilet paper. The toilet paper roll was removed from her cell, and she was told to ask for some when she needed it. She then defecated on the floor and proceeded to smear stool over the windows and all over the floor and walls of her cell. She was asked to clean up her cell by giving her paper towels and cleanser, to which she refused. Instead, she continued to defecate on the floor and further smear the feces all over her cell. The odor became so intense, all other inmates had to be removed from the cells in that area. Three staff volunteered to be the cleanup crew. Summer was removed from the cell so it could be cleaned. It wasn't long before she did it all over again.

Summer's number of write-ups included assault on staff, disorderly conduct, destruction of property, and cheeking medications (hiding them in her mouth but not taking them). These are only a few of the too many to mention issues during Summer's incarceration.

When Summer's prison sentence finally came to an end, she was paroled to the state hospital.

JESSIE

Jessie was the firstborn daughter in her family. She had a brother who was born seven years before Jessie. It was difficult to get Jessie to open up about her childhood. But one day during a routine blood draw, she was very melancholy and quiet. She was ready to talk and told me that her father was very abusive. She said he would go off without warning or any apparent reason. He took out his anger on both Jessie and her mother. He rarely ever laid a hand on his pride and joy, his son, Tommy. Tommy was much older than Jessie, so he was almost never home to witness the abuse of his little sister. Tommy moved out of the family home when Jessie was eleven. When Tommy left, Jessie felt she had lost her only friend.

Jessie's mother was an alcoholic like her father. She made Jessie feel like she was always in the way. Both parents made countless comments about the burden their daughter was for them. Her mother seemed to enjoy belittling Jessie. She often told her daughter that she was stupid and as worthless as a piece of garbage. The children at school frequently teased Jessie because her clothes were dirty and torn and because she smelled bad.

It didn't take long until Jessie decided that enough was enough. She was no longer going to be bullied by anyone. It was time to fight back. She was full of pain and humiliation from all the years of abuse from her parents and the kids at school. She felt she was about to explode. The abused became the abuser. She began getting into trouble at school regularly until she was suspended and finally kicked out of school at fifteen years old. That last day of school ended with her father beating her with his belt. Then she snapped. She got hold of his belt, held it in the air, and screamed at the top of her lungs that it was over and he would never hit her again. She swung the belt with fifteen years of fury and pain. The belt whipped through the air with all her might and slashed across the left side of his face. He looked at her in utter shock with blood running down his face. Her father had been left with a deep, four-inch gash across his left cheek. It was a permanent scar as a reminder of the last time he ever laid eyes on his daughter. After her mother put her father in the car and drove off to the emergency room, Jessie took off with nothing but the clothes on her back. As she ran out the back door and down the driveway, she suddenly stopped. She turned around and went back into the house and into her parents' bedroom. She slid open the top drawer of their nightstand, reached under the phone book, and grabbed her father's handgun. She stared at the shiny black pistol, which felt smooth and cool against her skin. The gun gave her the feeling of strength she desperately needed. As she tucked the gun in her waistband at her back, she whispered to herself that no one will ever fuck with her again. She ran and never looked back.

Jessie was homeless and lived on the streets for years. She stole, robbed, and did whatever it took just to survive. She went through garbage cans behind restaurants to eat. Then she prostituted her body and sold drugs for money.

Jessie finally found her brother, Tommy. He was working at a garage changing oil and tires and doing car repairs. Tommy let her sleep on his couch so she had a roof over her head.

Tommy had a girlfriend, Rita, who also lived at the apartment. Rita waited tables at a nearby pizza joint. Jessie hated Rita, and the feeling was mutual. The two women argued constantly. Jessie felt Rita was using her brother and was cheating on him. She wanted Rita gone. One night, Tommy had to finish repairs on a car at the shop. He told Jessie it would take most of the night and asked her if she would take Rita's car and pick her up from work at the restaurant at midnight when she got off. Jessie was pissed but said she'd do it for his sake. At 12:10 a.m., Rita walked out of the restaurant and got in the car. She asked Jessie why the fuck she was driving her car. Then the fight began. Jessie drove to an empty parking lot and stopped the car. She told Rita that she was a whore and didn't deserve Tommy. When Rita asked her what she was going to do about it, Jessie reached inside her backpack and pulled out her father's gun. She pointed the gun at Rita's chest and simply said, "This." Jessie fired the gun twice into Rita's rib cage. Rita screamed in agony. Jessie started the car, drove to a bar a few blocks away, and parked. Rita opened the car door and fell to the ground, screaming. She crawled on the street to the back of the car, trying to get away with her life. Jessie got out of the car and walked to where Rita was lying bleeding all over the pavement. Jessie snapped. She yelled that Rita got what she deserved and began kicking her in the stomach, releasing a pent-up fury from deep within. By this time, a crowd was gathering around from inside the bar witnessing this horrifying scene. No one stepped in to stop Jessie; everyone froze. Jessie suddenly stopped, got in Rita's car, and drove away. Jessie was apprehended eight hours later. Rita died on the street in a pool of blood.

Jessie was sentenced to life in prison without the chance for parole.

Jessie's rage had turned her into a completely different person. It became clear that she was a force to be reckoned with. Every inmate found out quick upon their arrival at the prison that Jessie was top dog. Nobody messes with the top dog.

Jessie served her time, knowing how to manipulate the staff and the correctional system to get what she wanted. In women's prisons, women tend to immediately build relationships with other women. It's a fact proven over and over in correctional systems. But not Jessie. She was completely antisocial and never had a single woman she called a friend in her twenty years of incarceration. She did mellow somewhat by this point. For the last five years of the twenty served, she stayed out of trouble and kept herself busy with solitary arts and crafts and other projects.

The time to appear before the parole board had arrived. Jessie was confident that she'd get parole this time. Twenty years served, good behavior, and the fact she was fifty-nine years old had to be her ticket to the outside.

On the morning of her hearing, she appeared before the board with hopes high. Jessie pled her case for release. However, the board members comments to her were cold, heartless, and even cruel. They told her that despite how she had behaved the twenty years she served, her crime was brutal, violent, and unforgivable. The board denied her parole quickly and without a doubt. They told Jessie to not even think about applying for parole for at least another fifteen years. She would be seventy-four years old.

Two days later, Jessie attempted suicide by hanging. She had everything planned out for a fifteen-minute time frame where she wouldn't be missed. When facilitywide formal count indicated she was unaccounted for, an officer on her first day at the prison ran to the storage room where Jessie worked. Jessie was found hanging from a tall steel storage rack with a bathrobe belt tied around her neck. Emergency calls were heard throughout the facility. Jessie was cut down, and CPR was immediately started. Air was not going into her lungs despite numerous position changes and attempts. It was found that Jessie had made the extra attempt for successful suicide by placing a tight rubber band beneath the bathroom tie around her throat. The band was deep, and the swelling around her neck, hid the fact that it was there. Once it was found and cut, the nurse was able to provide good ventilations, and Jessie's lungs filled with air. The paramedics arrived and took over attempts to revive her. I was able to access a vein in her foot to give IV fluids and necessary drugs while the paramedics worked to start a secondary IV in her arms and neck. Then they placed her on a mechanical chest compressions machine to make her heart pump. Once the drugs were in, Jessie's heart began to beat on its own. She was transported to a nearby hospital by ambulance with the nurse at her side. Her heart stopped twice on the transport, and CPR was resumed. Again and again, she was brought back. She was then flown to a major medical center, where she was pronounced dead. Her brain had gone without oxygen for too long.

Jessie had disowned all living family, but she had a directive for her lawyer to take her ashes and spread them in the lake where she had found solace and comfort.

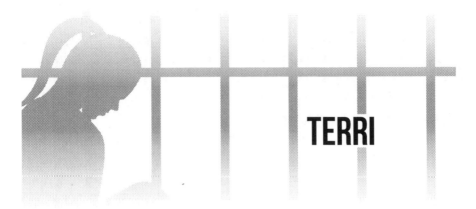

TERRI

Terri was one of the younger inmates who always found a way to be in trouble. She spent many days and nights in the hole. Most of the time, it was for fighting with another inmate, and not just verbally because she knew how to throw some serious punches to the face. She also wasn't afraid to assault staff for not getting her way, or even just because she was having a bad day. Terri was another frequent flyer at the prison. It was never long after her release before she'd be back at our doors.

Something that is so amazing to see after working in a prison for fifteen years is watching the young inmates grow up. Studies have indicated that when young girls start using drugs, their brain development slows way down. It's been said that many of the women incarcerated have the mentality of a fourth grader; that was often when they started using meth and other drugs.

Terri was one of those girls. Over the years, I watched Terri change. Usually, her admission process was dealing with a very angry teenager. Today, Terri came back to us again, but this time was very different.

I visited with her quite a while before she went in for her admission physical at doctor call. She was smiling from ear to ear. I asked her why she was back in prison again. She said before she left here the last time, she had to provide an address to parole to. Tiffany, a former inmate, willingly offered Terri a place to stay with her. But when Terri got there, Tiffany had no intention of letting Terri live with her. So she had no family, no friends, and nowhere to go. She had to live out of her car. It wasn't too bad until the weather turned to winter, and freezing temperatures made living in a car miserable. Finding a place to park was trying because police were always telling her to move on. It was scary too. One night when she was trying to get some sleep, some men started banging on her windows with their fists and yelling that they were going to get her.

Then, one night while driving around at 1:00 a.m., she was pulled over by police. She said she had a baggie of meth, which she quickly put it in her vagina. She was taken to jail for possession of paraphernalia. Terri said she was so relieved to get three meals a day and a warm bed. But when she found out she wasn't going to be placed in custody in a halfway house or prison, she was faced with becoming homeless again, and winter was just getting started. She knew she had to act, so she removed the meth from her vagina and made sure the officers found it. They did. Terri was sent back to prison.

Talking with Terri was like meeting a totally different person than the one I knew. This Terri was very mature, calm, and happy to be here. She would be safe, warm, and fed. And she knew that this would be a truly Merry Christmas. No matter how small, she knew she would receive a gift of warm socks, gloves, or something special, and she would get a big Christmas dinner.

Thinking about what Terri went through, when I go home every night with everything I could possibly want, made me sad. So many of the women here never really had a chance at a good life. Reading their background stories of alcoholic and drug-addicted parents and the abuse, both sexual and physical, was hard to imagine. There was never the chance of a college education or meeting a good man who would treat them right. Somehow, the circle of addiction and abuse seemed to continue over and over through each generation.

RAINBOW

Rainbow looked like a middle-aged housewife. She was very quiet. She had long brown hair, glasses, and a tiny body frame. You almost felt sorry for her. She was going to be here a very long time. Rainbow called police and told them that her son had passed on. When police arrived, Rainbow was sitting on the couch with the dead child on her lap. She had no expression on her face and did not shed a single tear. CPR had not been given. The teenage boy's mouth could not be opened to give breaths because rigor mortise had already set in. The teenage boy weighed a mere twenty pounds—the weight of a toddler. His bones stuck out and there were bruises over much of his body. This poor boy appeared to have been beaten and had been starved to death by his own mother. Rainbow was charged with murder.

SAGE

Sage came to prison with a bad attitude and a huge chip on her shoulder. She never smiled. Sage had lost the will to live. She was addicted to drugs and felt completely hopeless. With one look at Sage, I felt a true sense of compassion. Sometimes staff can become hardened in this environment, and compassion can be hard to find when inmates are calling you names and spitting in your face. What's more, showing compassion can be perceived by an inmate as something much more and something very different than intended. It can be very difficult for nurses trained to show compassion to their patients in a correctional environment. Nurses must be kind but professional with the incarcerated women at all times.

Sage was twenty-five years old. She was very petite with jet-black hair and dark eyes. But it were her hands that drew my attention. She had the hands of a ninety-year-old crippled woman. Her medical assessment showed her feet to be just as bad. She had the worst case of rheumatoid arthritis I had ever seen.

Her troubles with the law and eventual imprisonment had begun years ago. Sage had turned to drugs in part to help her deal with her constant, excruciating pain. She had doctored many years, but either she couldn't tolerate the side effects of the medications prescribed, or they didn't help her pain and suffering.

By the time she reached the doors of our medical department for her initial medical assessment, she had resigned herself to giving up on life completely. She spoke about her daughter, who she said meant the world to her, but still felt she had no hope of living a normal life.

I met with Sage several times and asked her to let us help her. Each time, she said she couldn't go through all the testing and medications that made her so sick all over again. I'm not sure why, but on another teary afternoon, she asked to see me and agreed to let us try to help her.

Through lots of paperwork and multiple requests, we finally obtained permission from the state department of corrections to provide Sage the costly medications necessary to treat her disease. She was sent to physical and occupational therapy for evaluation and treatments that included paraffin (hot wax) treatments prior to therapy sessions and custom-made hand splints to keep her joints from dislocating themselves. Although her feet were small in length, her crippled bone structures did not fit in a regular shoe, so she was sent to a podiatrist foot specialist and was custom-fitted with shoes that had a large toe box for her. She was sent to arthritis specialists and bone specialists as well.

As the weeks went by, I began noticing how she was quick to give me a big smile, and she went out of her way to say hello when she met me in the halls of the prison.

Almost eight months to the day from her arrival, Sage came to the infirmary to take one of her shots for her treatment. I heard her crying as she met with our physician's assistant. Afterward, she asked to speak with me. She stepped into my office with tears rolling down her face. She told me about how happy she was that I had taken the time and made the effort to help her. She thanked me and the nursing staff for saving her life and giving her a second chance at a future.

ROSE

One day in March 2016, we booked Rose, a native woman in her early forties. She came in with an above-the-knee amputation that was a result of repeated MRSA infections that had caused her to lose her leg several years ago. She stood at a very tall six feet and had good upper body strength from the use of the wheelchair and crutches. She arrived at the prison on a torrential amount of pain pills with doses higher than our nurses had ever seen. Needless to say, many of the drugs she was on were not allowed in prison. The morphine, clonazepam, and several others had to be stopped immediately because they are banned in correctional facilities.

Rose threw a fit, wrote grievances (a formal process that allows inmates to have something they disagree with, addressed to me as the director of the medical department), and complained to anyone who would listen to try to get her drugs reinstated. It didn't work. Over time, she began to settle down. Then we found out that in addition to the high doses of ibuprofen we were giving her every day, she was purchasing an excessive amount from commissary and trading her food items for more. She was risking an overdose and organ damage. Despite verbal warnings to stop, her commissary orders for ibuprofen blocked, and signing a contract with medical to take ibuprofen only as it was ordered, she continued to borrow from other inmates and take extremely dangerous amounts. She received a write-up for having concealed a large amount of ibuprofen under her pillow, and she ended up housed in the infirmary to monitor her and keep her safe. She wasn't happy, but she did cooperate—until she was served the write-up. Her sanction for concealing the ibuprofen was to lose the television provided for her in the infirmary cell. She was furious.

About an hour after she was served the write-up, CO Mattson knocked on her door to announce lunchtime, looked through her window, and stated, "What are you doing?" I immediately followed CO Mattson and entered Rose's cell. She was in her wheelchair with her back to the door and was slumped forward. As I came around her chair, I saw a large pool of blood on the floor with a big area of clotted blood. Her clothing and body were covered in blood. I ran across the infirmary and grabbed gloves and gauze dressings. I ran back into Rose's cell and tried to see where all the blood was coming from. I saw a large gash with blood dripping from it across her left wrist and a smaller gash next to it. As I applied pressure with the gauze, I asked her what she had used to do this. Her eyes were open, but she would not respond. It was then that I noticed more deep lacerations to her right wrist, and both inner aspects of her elbows. CO Mattson appeared to be in shock as she stood staring at all the blood and not moving. I shoved gauze in CO Mattson's hand and yelled to provide pressure over the wounds on the right arm while I pushed down on both injuries on the left arm. Prior to applying pressure, CO Mattson announced the emergency over the prison radio and told Control to call 911 for an ambulance.

As more staff began arriving, Rose came to life and began fighting against us as we worked to hold her down and save her life. Despite the large blood loss, Rose had the strength of a lion. She fought against us, yelling, "Let me die! Let me die!" She was not about to stop resisting, despite the trained hands of the COs as they applied pressure points, attempting control of her. I yelled, above the inmate's hollering, for the other nurse to grab me rolls of gauze to wrap her wounds. Rose was now calling all the staff vulgar names. "You fucking bitch! Bring it on, you fucking pieces of shit! C'mon! Hurt me! You think you're so tough? I'm gonna sue your fucking asses for hurting my shoulder!"

I was struggling seven minutes into this. The pain from my lower back was screaming at me. But I remained bent over, holding tight to her wounds and desperately trying to stop the bleeding. I called for the restraint chair. While we waited for the restraint chair to be brought to the infirmary, five staff lifted Rose up into her wheelchair. As we tried to maintain pressure on her wounds and wheel her out of her cell, Rose forced her body to slide out of the wheelchair and onto the floor.

We feverishly struggled to pick her up while Rose continued to fight us. The four COs and I dragged her out of the cell, slipping and sliding on her trail of blood. We got her out of the cell and placed her in the restraint chair. Once in the chair, we were able to restrain all three limbs and better apply pressure dressings to her wounds. Despite the blood loss, she continued screaming profanities to staff. We wheeled her down the hall to Control, where the ambulance team would be entering. Handcuffs were applied on top of her bandaged wrists. The ambulance team arrived moments later. Two large maintenance men picked her up and laid her on the gurney, where she was fully strapped down again.

I watched as the ambulance team and two of our officers drove away to the hospital emergency room.

Nurses are taught to react with their training in emergency situations and not feel at the time. We often do this routinely when seriously demanding events like this occur. The severity of what had just taken place didn't register in my mind until I returned to the infirmary and looked around. It looked like a war scene from a movie. I observed the wide smear of blood and blood-soaked gauze that went from the inmate's cell across the infirmary's white tile to the restraint chair, where Rose had fought us kicking and screaming as we struggled to save her life. Inside her cell were pools of blood. I searched to find what she used to cause the deep lacerations. I found a broken razor blade in the blood, and nearby was a shaving razor with the blades removed. Blood was everywhere, including on most staff who were involved. Luckily, this inmate was HIV and hepatitis C negative.

Hours later, I was notified at home that inmate Rose required a great deal of sedation in the emergency room so the physicians could suture her multiple wounds. She continued fighting the doctors and nurses until the sedation took hold and put her to sleep. The end result was twelve staples to her wrists as well as an additional sixty-eight sutures to close her wounds. Once Rose was stabilized, she was transferred to the state hospital and admitted for mental health treatment.

The investigation regarding the event could only summarize that Rose attempted suicide because her television was taken away for several days due to an infraction she had committed a few days earlier.

Ten days after the suicide attempt, Rose was returned to our facility and placed on suicide observation. Two days later, she argued with nursing staff, stating they weren't giving her the right drugs. She demanded medications that were not allowed in prison. An hour after yelling at the staff, she remained quietly underneath her suicide smock, refusing to comply with keeping her head out from under the blanket and responding to staff that she was okay during hourly checks on her well-being. When security staff entered the cell, it was found that Rose had torn off the Steri-Strips and, using her fingers, dug into her wounds, ripping them open with her fingers. She was placed in the restraint chair so her wounds could be redressed and she could be kept from further harm. I asked Rose if she would let us restitch her wounds, and she refused, stating, "No! If you do, I'll just rip them open again and again!"

Rose kept her word. She was found multiple times digging deeply past the first joint of her finger inside her inner elbow wounds to the bone. Her face was without any emotion, and she appeared almost peaceful while she repetitively reopened her wounds.

This process took place multiple times in the next few weeks. She finally stopped self-harming, took her medications, complied with staff, and was returned to minimum-security housing. For four weeks, she seemed to be doing quite well. But on one cold afternoon in December, an emergency in the minimum-security housing showers was announced over the prison radio. I arrived with my medical bag along with several officers to find inmate Rose sitting dressed in her wheelchair in the shower, her clothes soaked with her own blood and a razor blade in her hand. She had cut open both wrists and both inner elbows again, and she was trying to cut her throat when the officer found her, stopped her, and activated the emergency announcement. Everything went from there as it had just a few short weeks before. Her reason for attempted suicide this time? She later told staff if was because her kids weren't answering the phone when she called.

Once stabilized again, Rose received parole to the state hospital.

I never saw Rose again. This was yet another case of forever wondering what happened to this inmate.

DAKOTA

I did the medical admission on an unforgettable nineteen-year-old girl named Dakota. With a very serious face, she told me that she had a four-year-old daughter named Daisy. I asked her where her daughter was. She said some pirates had taken her, and she was on their ship somewhere at sea. Part of the blood-draw questionnaire asked how many sex partners she had been with. She said she had never had sex with a man in her life. I asked her if her daughter was adopted, to which she replied no; she had given birth to the child. The interview got more confusing. When I asked her what her religion was, she replied, "Huffing." I tried to rephrase and ensure that she knew what I was asking her, but her response was the same. Huffing. I finally asked her if she knew where she was and why. She did. She said she was at prison, and it was because she had stolen a car. She had stolen a car, all right. I later found out that she had been arrested, and when the sheriff's deputy went into a gas station, Dakota had somehow managed to get behind the wheel of the deputy's car and drive away. I can't imagine how this took place, but the look on the deputy's face when he went outside to find his missing car must have been priceless. Dakota was found with the missing deputy's car later that day.

Dakota had a history of drug abuse but did a great deal of huffing chemicals. We could only assume that was at least part of her apparent brain damage. She was soon taken under the wing of very large black woman named Jada, whom most of the inmates feared. Jada was very loud and had a following of several other ladies. Dakota became one of many. Jada told Dakota that she would cheek her medications and give them to Dakota to get high in return for sex. Dakota agreed. Three months later, Dakota took all the pills Jada had been cheeking at one time. She was later found unresponsive on the floor by her bed and was sent to the hospital by ambulance. Her stomach was pumped, and she was given a charcoal substance through the tube into her stomach to bind to the drugs and save her from the overdose. Dakota was in a coma. Her kidneys shut down, and she was placed on dialysis. Her lungs shut down, and she was placed on a ventilator to breathe. She nearly faced death.

Dakota was in and out of a coma and hospitalized for three months before her return to prison. Jada didn't cheek any more of her meds, at least not for Dakota.

Dakota was always getting in trouble and receiving write-ups. She was very immature for her age, possibly due to drug use that started when she was very young. Girls' development stops at the onset of regular drug use. Testing on twenty-year-old women who began their history of drug use in the fourth grade often showed they had the maturity of a ten-year-old, even in adulthood. This was exactly how Dakota presented. She was frequently acting out in a childish manner in the GED classroom. She couldn't focus on the tasks assigned to her, and she would misbehave and get kicked out by the teacher for disrupting the entire class. Other days, she would refuse to go to GED because she wanted to sleep or just didn't feel like it. In large group entertainment events, it was more of the same. She couldn't stay seated in her chair, she would throw spitballs of paper at other girls, and she couldn't stop talking. During an STD women's health class that I taught, Dakota giggled every time I used words like *vagina*, *penis*, and *intercourse*. Despite multiple warnings from me and other students shushing her, I had to have security remove her, and she received yet another write-up for her behavior. While standing in line for lunch, she would pull girls' hair. In the IDR, she'd steal other girls' food. She was bouncing off the walls much of the time. In this correctional facility, no attention deficit medications were allowed. One of the reasons was because the risk of abuse was so high. A girl with this disorder is calmed and allowed to focus better on this drug, whereas those without this diagnosis could attain a high from it. Some inmates would bully the girl on the drug to get her to cheek it and give it to them. Other girls on these medications would cheek and sell it due to the high demand for it. Therefore, the department of corrections chose to weigh the risks and benefits and completely ban the drug. However, in extreme cases, this could be overturned. Dakota was not at a real risk to herself or others without the drug and therefore was denied. She was just a handful.

DIANA

Diana was a bit of a surprise on her arrival to the prison. Normally, we see inmates walk in with just handcuffs and a black-and-white jail jumpsuit. But not Diana. She arrived with each wrist cuffed to a wheelchair as well as both ankles shackled to the chair as well, and a spit hood over her head. She looked like someone in a horror movie.

County jail staff report that Diana has a very violent history. In the county jail where she was housed, Diana was assaultive toward inmates and staff. She was confined in a solitary cell due to her violent behavior toward anyone and everyone. Diana reportedly would be speaking very calmly and then suddenly strike out for no known reason. An inmate who was housed in the same county jail with Diana remarked how she was scared of the "inmate chained to the wheelchair."

Diana was taken to the infirmary for the medical portion of her admission process. She seemed to be comfortable with the nurse doing her admission. Nurse Alice was a young, pretty, and soft-spoken correctional nurse. Diana answered some of the health history questions appropriately, but it took only moments to realize just how delusional Diana was. She kept repeating many of the same things over and over. For example, when Alice asked her if she had any children, she quickly stated, "Yes, I was raped. The judge raped me. He raped my children!" Then she said, "They're trying to poison me ... water has poison in it ..." Alice obtained what health history she could, and we decided to place Diana in SMU until she could be better assessed and we could keep her and everyone else around her safe.

The strangest thing about Diana, besides her delusions, was her hazy blue eyes. Sometimes she would look at you, but it didn't feel like she was even looking at you. It was as if she could see right through you. It's difficult to explain, but it was disconcerting. Her gaze was initially like a deer in the headlights but could quickly change to a Charlie Manson glare.

The day we had Diana scheduled for a blood draw, she appeared to be calm and in a good mood. Two officers escorted the inmate to the medical department. Because Diana seemed to like Alice, we decided Alice was to do the blood draw with me assisting her. Diana arrived in full restraints. After Alice explained exactly what she was going to do, she inserted the needle into Diana's right arm. She was having some difficulty cannulating the vein. Suddenly, Diana jerked her arm back, nearly sticking Alice with the dirty needle. Before security staff could act, Diana jumped off the exam table and swung her handcuffed fists at Alice, hitting her in the face and sending her flying over a chair and into the wall. While the staff gained control of the inmate, I helped the shaken Alice to her feet. The officers quickly took the cussing and screaming Diana out of the infirmary and locked her down in the SMU. Diana would receive a write-up with sanctions, including loss of several privileges and a lengthy stay in lockdown, and she would be charged with assault. As for Alice, she ended up with a black eye, a lump on the back of her head, and later, a letter of resignation on my desk.

Assault on staff rarely happened in this facility, especially when full restraints and two trained security officers were in place. But in this kind of environment, it could happen. There was never room for complacence. Training for all staff was frequently held, and we must always remember where we were.

LYDIA

Lydia had been an inmate at this prison multiple times. Her most recent crime involved possession of a controlled substance. She stated she "tried meth for the first time and went crazy." While at the county jail awaiting sentencing, she got out of her handcuffs, managed to get into the kitchen without being seen, grabbed a large kitchen knife, and stabbed an officer in the chest. Luckily, he was treated and released from the hospital. On another day, while at a medical appointment at a clinic, Lydia got out of her cuffs a second time and escaped. An initial possession charge changed into something much more. At her court date, she was sentenced to ten years in prison. She tried to fight this with an appeal, and her reason was "she was dying." The truth was she did have HIV and AIDS. She also had a diagnosis of hepatitis C, which was later treated at the prison until no levels of the deadly virus could be detected. She was cured. This treatment cost the prison ninety thousand dollars. When Lydia went to her court hearing, the judge upheld her sentence to remain at ten years.

Lydia was a medical nightmare, always complaining of one physical ailment or another. She was frequently seen at sick call and doctor call with complaints right out of a textbook. The librarian reported that Lydia checked out medical books from the library two to three times weekly. This made sense when she had all the symptoms of strange diseases like malaria, typhoid fever, and more.

During medline one evening, Stacy, Lydia's dorm mate, asked if she could talk to me in private. Once medline ended, I called Stacy to my office. She told me that something was going to go down. She went on to say that she had overheard Lydia talking to her girlfriend the other night. The inmates were in the bathroom and thought they were alone. Lydia told her friend Margaret that she had a plan to escape. She went on to say that she was going to fake an illness serious enough that would result in a trip to the ER. With just two security officers guarding her, Lydia said she'd find a way to slip out and run.

After Stacy left my office, I informed the chief of security of what I was told. She then informed all the captains to be extra observant.

Two weeks later, Lydia attended a class that was held for any inmates interested in better parenting. (Lydia didn't have any children.) She started coughing and told the case manager that she wasn't feeling well, so the case manager walked her to the stairway to her housing unit so she could go to her room and lie down. Moments later, the case manager came over the radio and intercom requesting medical staff and security assistance. We found Lydia at the bottom of the stairs lying face down. I advised security staff not to attempt to move her. Her face was a dark purple color. As more staff arrived, we carefully rolled her onto her back while supporting her neck in case of a fracture. She was not breathing. Medical staff immediately obtained an oxygen tank and Ambu bag, and we began rescue breathing for her. Her pulse was thready and weak, but it was there. She began breathing, so we stopped rescue breathing and watched her oxygen level on the pulse oximeter. Her blood oxygen levels began dropping again, and she was gasping and struggling to breathe, so we resumed rescue breathing. Then we lost her pulse. As we cut off her shirt and prepared the automatic defibrillator (AED), we started chest compressions. After multiple compressions, she opened her eyes. She had a pulse. We stopped compressions, and she was breathing better on her own. We continued giving her a flow of oxygen and reassured the fear in her eyes that everything was going to be okay. At this time, the ambulance crew arrived and took her to the ER at the local hospital.

Upon her return to the prison, it was documented by the ER physician that her final diagnosis was a headache. It was true that she had a resulting headache and bump on her head once she got to the ER, along with a sore ankle from her fall down half the stairwell.

We ordered a set of diagnostics to try to find the cause of what had happened, including forty-eight-hour Holter heart monitor, EKG, and a full cardiology workup. Every test came back normal. Lydia told me that she didn't remember anything that had happened that day. I couldn't help but wonder if this fall was planned but resulted in more than was intended.

CAROLINE

On a Friday evening, shortly before count, Caroline was yelling at her roommates in dorm 7. Someone had stolen much of her commissary, including her coffee and candy bars. When CO Barry entered the dorm and asked what was all the yelling was about, one could have heard a pin drop. No one would say anything. That was how it worked. No matter what the issues were, inmates never told the "screws." They handled problems on their own. After supper, when Caroline went to the bathroom, her roommates were waiting for her. While Tammy stood at the bathroom door on watch for the guards, Tina (the dorm boss) and two of the other girls had filled a sink plugged with a towel and full of water. They grabbed Caroline and dragged her to the sink. Tina told Caroline that she needed to learn a lesson. She told her that she owned all commissary that was in the dorm and that Caroline had better learn that quickly. They shoved Caroline's face below the water and held her down. When Caroline struggled to the surface and tried to scream, choking on the water, the girls forced her back down again and again. When she became limp and stopped fighting, they dropped her lifeless body to the bathroom floor. The inmates walked back to their dorm, talking and laughing all the way. When inmate Susie found Caroline on the bathroom floor barely breathing, she ran for the officer in the security office.

Later in the infirmary, Captain Caleb asked Caroline what had happened. All she would say over and over was that she had slipped in the water on the bathroom floor. She was kept in the medical department overnight under observation. The next morning, Caroline returned to her dorm. Nothing was said, and that was the end of it. Lesson learned.

Caroline lay in her bed and remembered another time when she had almost drowned. That time, she was choking on her own vomit. She didn't remember most of it, but she never forgot the events because her seven-year-old sister had told her what had happened.

It was four years ago, when she was seventeen. She was hooked on OxyContin. One evening after another fight with her mother, her mom left to work a twelve-hour night shift at the hospital. Caroline complained to her mother that there was nothing for her and Ava to eat in the house. She asked her mother for twenty-five dollars to order pizza and wings. After her mom left for work, Caroline made a peanut butter and jelly sandwich and gave it to Ava, who was busy coloring in her room. Caroline then called her dealer, Zeke. Twenty minutes later, Zeke pulled up in a rusted-out Camaro. She climbed inside and exchanged the money for a baggie of Oxy. She went into the bathroom, closed the door, and took six of the pills. She was so angry and fed up with all the arguing all the time. She dumped the rest of the pills into her hand, swallowed them, and lay down on the floor, staring at the ceiling.

What happened next, Caroline doesn't remember, but Ava will never forget. Ava was still coloring in her Barbie coloring book when she heard noises coming from the bathroom. She opened the door to find Caroline on her back with vomit on her shirt and the floor. Her mouth was full of vomit, and she was choking and gurgling. Her face was a blueish color, and Ava was terrified. She struggled to roll her sister on her side and clear the vomit from her mouth so she could breathe. Ava stayed by her sister's side until Caroline regained consciousness. The seven-year-old had saved Caroline's life that night.

MELANIE

This afternoon, we received multiple females for admission. They came in their issued jail uniforms of black and white stripes and faded oranges. Just another day, it seemed. As I observed the group of arrivals in the infirmary from my desk, I noticed one particular girl. She stood alone against the wall, shoulders hunched forward, her uniform barely hanging from her thin frame. Her eyes looked so sunken and hollow. It wasn't just the dark circles beneath her eyes. It was something else. She wasn't defiant, sarcastic, and giggling immaturely like the rest of the girls she came in with. This one had seen some rough times, I felt in my gut.

We don't always know what crimes these women come to prison for. Most of the time, we do. Other times, we really wish we didn't know.

Melanie's story is a sad one. Her father began molesting her and raped her by the age of six years old. Not long after the nightmare with her father began, her two brothers reached teenage years, and they began molesting her too. So many abused children end up in an abusive relationship when they grow up and leave their childhood home. That was exactly what Melanie did. She went for the first guy who paid attention to her and was willing to get her out of her family's home. It seemed like true love for a while, until he began threatening her and not allowing her to leave the trailer house. Then the beatings started. It wasn't long before all her front teeth had been knocked out, her eye socket was shattered by his fist, he cut her across the face with his hunting knife, and he punched her and kicked her in her pregnant belly, causing the death of their unborn child, a little girl. He never let her go to the doctor to sew up the gash on her face. He told her to tape up her ugly face so he didn't have to look at it. He also told her that she deserved to lose the damn kid since she had gotten herself pregnant in the first place. This was all in the first year they were together.

One cold October night, he came home from the bar extremely drunk, but not drunk enough to prevent him from taking out his anger on her. That night, he beat her until she was unconscious on the kitchen floor. Melanie woke up hours later in a pool of her own blood. One eye was swollen completely shut. With her other eye, she tried to look through the bleeding from the cut on her forehead. He was still passed out on the couch. She knew there was no time to find a coat and put on shoes. She slowly tried to stand, hanging onto the kitchen counter as she pulled herself. As she tried to take a step forward, it was all she could do to not scream in agony or make a single sound. The bones in her left shin were busted and coming through the skin. She vaguely remembered, through his punches earlier, that this was what he said would happen if she ever tried to leave him. She wiped the blood and tears from her eye and told herself that she could do this. She had to.

She gently lowered her body back to the floor. Using her hands and her one good leg, she began sliding herself toward the door. At that point, he let out a snort, and she froze. He continued snoring and breathing again. *Just a little farther,* she told herself. She managed to sneak through the old screen door and slowly lower her body down the rickety wood steps. The second step let out a loud squeak. She feared that noise would wake him. *It's over. He's going to kill her now for sure.* But there was silence. With hope in her heart, she continued through the mud that might've been green grass once upon a time. Her fingertips were ice cold and burning, but she continued until she got out into the middle of the street. As car lights approach, she frantically waved her hand in the air, hoping and praying the driver would come this way and see her. He did. It was an insurance man on his way to a town one hundred miles away. He took her to the hospital there, and her recovery began.

INMATE MEMOS FROM INMATES TO THE MEDICAL DEPARTMENT

Marissa writes, "I need permission for a bottom bunk. My tailbone hurts when I climb up and down the bunk ladder. I had back labor with all three of my kids."

Susan sends a memo that says, "I need a pregnancy test. I haven't had my period for six months, and white stuff comes out my nipples if I pinch them really hard."

Cassie writes, "I've been so hungry since I got here. I've been holding my bowels to see if I wouldn't be so hungry. But now I'm constipated. Please help."

Lindsey writes, "I need to be seen for a bladder infection, or maybe it's an STD. I'm very uncomfortable. I think it's because they made me do four or five squats and coughs in the last six or seven days. Or maybe it's because I was diagnosed with trichomonas twenty months ago from having sex with the wrong guy. I didn't finish the treatment. And I haven't had sex with anybody since because the discharge is so gross and the smell is so awful!"

Patty says, "How come I got a memo telling me I don't have chlamydia or gonorrhea when I haven't even had a Pap test yet?" [These are tests done on urine.]

Keisha writes, "My leg hurts right here when I hit it." [Stop hitting it?]

Mandy writes, "I have been sharing a drink after Sarah D. She has an STD in her throat. Is it contagious? Please let me know." [Chlamydia and gonorrhea testing is with a urine test, and it is not generally found in one's throat.]

Ashley writes, "I haven't gotten my period, my stomach is blowing up, I'm throwing up, and my boobs hurt. Oh, and I'm sleeping a lot." [I don't think there's a protocol for those symptoms.]

Simone says, "I was seen for my cold and given Mucinex. But I'm not better. My nose is still sore and crusty, and I can't even pick my nose."

Bailey writes, "I have sores in my nose again that hurt and stink. Also, my finger hurts really bad."

Stephanie writes, "Can I get a sling for my arm? I had a radio [radial] head fracture before I came here."

Lauryn writes, "Ever since I got my tooth pulled, I've been having weird shooting and aching pains in my knees. It's so bad in the mornings, I can barely walk. [Dental work generally doesn't affect the knees.]

Bethany writes, "I have bad anxiety, and my chest hurts, so I've been going outside to get fresh air. But I also have humidity phobia. It promotes my PTSD and makes me miss my long life by law marriage to my husband and boyfriend. He's dead now. Can I have an aspirin?"

Heather says, "I have a sensitive issue. For the past three and a half weeks, I've noticed that my left labia has been swollen … when I touch it, it feels like a testicle sack. I'm confused."

Olivia's memo to the medical department states, "I was shoveling snow, and when I turned to dump the snow, I heard a pop in my wrist, and all of a sudden my hand went limp. It's dead now."

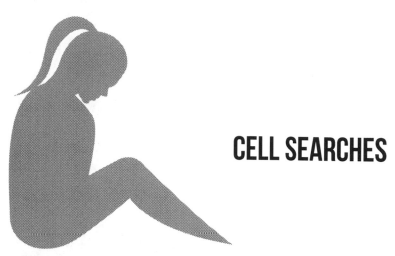

CELL SEARCHES

During a routine cell search, the on-duty captain found one inmate was apparently into arts and crafts. She had collected various Jolly Rancher candies and was able to heat the candy in the microwave and shape them without getting caught by a CO. After many attempts, she had succeeded in making a very large lollipop of many colors in the shape of a dildo, and it was found being passed around in the activity room.

After another search, the captain brought an item pulled from a dorm search to the medical department for identification of stolen property. Inmate Marybeth had stolen one of our disposable exam gloves and stuffed the middle finger with markers and tampons to make herself a dildo. This was confirmed by the inmate herself.

Lucille's cell search resulted in the finding of a plastic Pepsi bottle with a clear liquid in it that appeared to be water. Upon opening the bottle, the inmate had poured pure bleach into it. Bleach is a controlled substance in prison and is never allowed to be used, even in a diluted mixture of a ten to one, unless supervised by staff. Pure bleach thrown in someone's eyes can do some serious damage. When asked why she had it, she said that she liked to get up at night and scrub the floor around her bed with a washcloth.

As my day ends, I sign out, make my way through the pouring rain to my car, and head for home. I think about all the women who did their time at the prison. Some inmates will leave here with the tools given to them to succeed on the outside. Others will revert back to their old ways with a life of crime.

The sun peeks out from behind the thunder clouds, and a rainbow appears. Tomorrow is another day. And tomorrow and each day after it, I will do my best to be a positive influence and make a difference for these women as a nurse behind bars.

COVID-19

All contact visits at the prisons were suspended in March, 2020. Legal visits were also suspended but could be arranged via teleconference. In June 2020, the state began to phase in limited restricted visits. The adult prison stopped visits in July.

Mass COVID-19 testing was conducted on the entire inmate population and all staff. The largest dorm in the facility was cleared and used as the quarantine unit for all new inmate arrivals for fourteen days of daily body temperature checks and daily assessments by nursing staff. Any inmates who tested positive for COVID-19 were admitted to the infirmary and secured under lock and key on strict isolation. This included medical staff to wear specially fitted N95 masks, eye and face shields, gloves, and disposable gowns before opening the inmate cell door. Meals were provided with all disposable dishes and eating utensils and were disposed of in red isolation bags. All isolation bags were taken to a secured room and locked in an isolation safe. Finally, all isolation waste was picked up and destroyed by a contracted waste removal company.

All staff were required to take their body temperature and complete a COVID-19 questionnaire every day prior to entering the facility. The questionnaire asked if the staff member had any COVID-19 symptoms or had any exposure to anyone infected with the virus. The staff donned surgical masks before beginning their shift until their departure at the end of the day. These masks protected potential transmission to others but offered no protection for the person wearing the mask. Formal fit testing for all staff was conducted so N95 masks could be worn. The N95 masks offered two-way protection so the person wearing the mask was also protected. These masks made breathing somewhat difficult for the wearer and were also very warm.

No lives in the prison were lost due to the COVID-19 pandemic of 2020.

Printed in the United States
by Baker & Taylor Publisher Services